Fur Trader of the North

ALSO BY RONALD SYME

Alexander Mackenzie, Canadian Explorer
Amerigo Vespucci, Scientist and Sailor
Balboa, Finder of the Pacific
Benedict Arnold, Traitor of the Revolution
Bolívar, the Liberator
Captain Cook, Pacific Explorer
Captain John Paul Jones, America's Fighting Seaman
Cartier, Finder of the St. Lawrence
Champlain of the St. Lawrence
Columbus, Finder of the New World
Cortes of Mexico
De Soto, Finder of the Mississippi
First Man to Cross America
Francis Drake, Sailor of the Unknown Seas
Francisco Coronado and the Seven Cities of Gold
Francisco Pizarro, Finder of Peru
Frontenac of New France
Garibaldi, The Man Who Made a Nation
Henry Hudson
John Cabot and His Son Sebastian
John Smith of Virginia
La Salle of the Mississippi
Magellan, First Around the World
On Foot to the Arctic, The Story of Samuel Hearne
Quesada of Colombia
Sir Henry Morgan, Buccaneer
Toussaint, The Black Liberator
Vancouver, Explorer of the Pacific Coast
Vasco da Gama, Sailor Toward the Sunrise
Verrazano, Explorer of the Atlantic Coast
Walter Raleigh
William Penn, Founder of Pennsylvania
Zapata, Mexican Rebel
illustrated by William Stobbs

Juárez, The Founder of Modern Mexico
illustrated by Richard Cuffari

African Traveler, The Story of Mary Kingsley
Nigerian Pioneer, The Story of Mary Slessor
illustrated by Jacqueline Tomes

The Story of Pierre de la Verendrye

FUR TRADER
OF THE NORTH
by Ronald Syme

ILLUSTRATED BY RICHARD CUFFARI

William Morrow and Company

New York 1973

Printed in the United States of America.
Library of Congress Catalog Card Number 72-13603
ISBN 0-688-20076-1
ISBN 0-688-30076-6 (lib. bdg.)
1 2 3 4 5 77 76 75 74 73

Contents

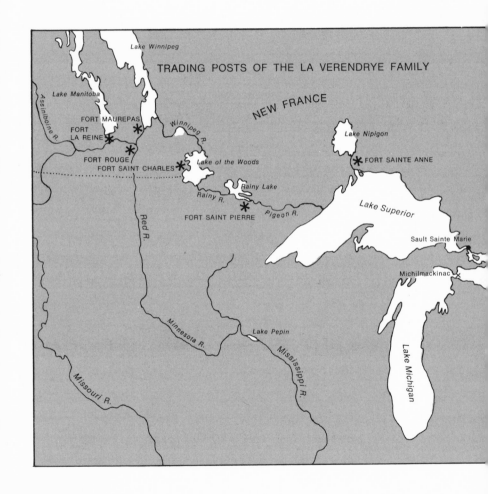

TRADING POSTS OF THE LA VERENDRYE FAMILY

Lake Winnipeg

Lake Manitoba

Assiniboine R.

Winnipeg R.

NEW FRANCE

FORT MAUREPAS
FORT
LA REINE

FORT ROUGE
FORT SAINT CHARLES

Lake of the Woods

Lake Nipigon

✳ FORT SAINTE ANNE

Rainy Lake

Rainy R.

Pigeon R.

FORT SAINT PIERRE

Lake Superior

Red R.

Sault Sainte Marie

Michilmackinac

Minnesota R.

Lake Pepin

Mississippi R.

Missouri R.

Lake Michigan

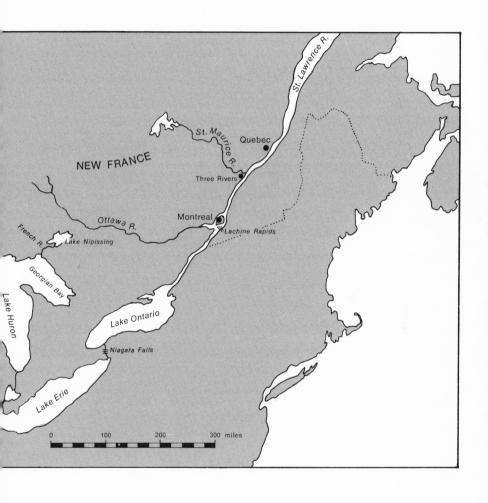

St. Lawrence R.

St. Maurice R.

Quebec

NEW FRANCE

Three Rivers

Ottawa R.

Montreal

Lachine Rapids

French R.

Lake Nipissing

Georgian Bay

Lake Huron

Lake Ontario

Niagara Falls

Lake Erie

0   100   200   300 miles

1
Growing Up

The French settlement of Three Rivers on the banks of the Saint Lawrence River was not a reassuring sight. Some 250 heavy-walled log cabins were scattered at irregular intervals along the northern bank of the river. They overlooked a rocky shore lapped by the deep, cold water. Behind them straggling fences and narrow ditches ran inland for the better part of a mile. There the dark and apparently endless forest began. The door of the little church was ironbound, and its narrow windows could be used as musket slits.

The two nearby windmills, which provided the people with freshly ground flour, also were intended for refuge in the event of an attack.

Pierre de la Verendrye (pronounced Vair-andre') was born at Three Rivers in 1685. His father was René Gaultier de la Verendrye, who had come to New France as a young lieutenant in the Army. By the time Lieutenant de la Verendrye's term of service ended, he had married Marie-Ursule Boucher, the daughter of the governor at Three Rivers, and he had grown to like his new way of life. When his father-in-law retired, he transferred his governorship to Lieutenant de la Verendrye.

The 400 settlers of Three Rivers formed a tough and adventurous community. Even the Iroquois left the settlement alone. On certain occasions in the past their warriors had attacked, but a number of their scalps had been nailed to log-cabin walls and left to blacken in the smoke of French tobacco pipes. In this environment of bullet molds, rough independence, and double-shotted muskets, young Pierre de la Verendrye spent his boyhood.

His father's position as governor of Three Rivers paid a salary of about $250 a year, which was little enough to support a wife and thirteen children, even in those days. Accordingly, Governor de la Verendrye decided to establish a fur-trading station. Named La Gabelle, it stood close to the Saint Maurice River, which flowed down from the north and joined the Saint Lawrence on the outskirts of Three Rivers. This trading post was situated handily and gave the governor first choice of all the furs brought in by friendly Indians.

At the age of fifty-five, which was as long as any man could reasonably expect to live in the climate and conditions of New France, Governor de la Verendrye died. His widow, a sturdy and shrewd woman, surveyed her financial position. La Gabelle was worth several hundred dollars a year, but there were signs that the natural supply of furs might begin to decrease soon. Thus, Madame de la Verendrye proceeded to sell the governership of Three Rivers for $1000. With four oxen, four cows, three sheep, a large number of hens, the usual cooking utensils, and

$175 in cash, she removed herself and her children to the Isle Dupas, close to Montreal, where her father had built a small farmhouse. While she and a couple of hired men set about developing the land, her son Pierre was packed off with his brothers and sisters to a small village school, which had been built recently on the southern bank of the river.

Life was hard and monotonous for the la Verendrye family, but it did them no harm. Cows and pigs had to be fed and tended during the long, bitter winter. Firewood had to be split, water drawn from the open-air pump, ice melted when the pump froze solid. Small game had to be shot or snared, tallow melted and made into candles, and the cooking pot, slung on a blackened chain above the large open fireplace, had to be filled daily in order to satisfy the appetites of the large and hungry family. Winter and summer alike, the hardworking and frugal Madame de la Verendrye made sure that her children were clad warmly and adequately fed.

There was little time for diversion or pleasure. In winter the surrounding landscape presented a dreary panorama of frozen fields, ice-covered river, stark black pine trees, and unbroken snow-fields. Things were better in the summer when the countryside turned green, flowers grew in the hedgerows, and canoes bearing friendly Indians or Frenchmen passed up and down the river.

Louis, the eldest boy, left for France in 1693, when he was twenty years old. "I have lived long enough with the forests and river," he told the envious eight-year-old Pierre. "In France I intend to join the Army. With our family name and assistance from our relatives, I may be able to obtain a commission."

Louis wrote from France the following year. He announced proudly that he was a second lieutenant and expecting promotion soon.

Pierre became even more envious. When he was twelve years old, he crossed the river in his canoe and volunteered as a cadet in the Montreal militia. A useful recruit, he was welcomed by the authorities.

Only five feet in height, Pierre was a lean, sandy-haired boy with gray eyes, sharp cheek-bones, and self-confidence instilled into him by his hard life on the farm. He could handle a musket or a canoe, trap, snare, and catch fish, look after himself in the forest, and cover long distances on snowshoes. Many boys several years older were not as tough.

The militia were not expected to practice the unthinking, mechanical drill of regular troops, to wear stiff and uncomfortable uniforms, or to carry out inexplicable maneuvers. They were simply guerrilla fighters, trained and knowledgeable in the ways of river and forest, men who could meet hostile Indians in their own type of warfare.

Pierre de la Verendrye became a militiaman. He was issued a musket, a blanket, a white cloak and cap, also a belt for the powder and shot horns and sheath knife, which he was expected to provide for himself.

Four years later, in 1701, France and England were at war. Called the War of the Spanish Succession in Europe, it was known as Queen Anne's War in the New World. Just as the American colonies, being ruled by England, were forced to enter this far-off conflict in which they had no active interest, so were the colonists of New France.

Orders came across the river to the Isle Dupas. Sixteen-year-old Pierre was to proceed downstream to Three Rivers and join a special militia force. Still, the important campaigns of his duty did not take place for several years.

Then the French governor-general of Canada persuaded the Abenaki Indians to take part in a hostile act against New England. Together with the Three Rivers militia, they were ordered to attack the English village of Deerfield, which lay close to the northern border of Massachusetts.

January of the year 1704 had arrived, and the whole countryside lay deep in the harshness of frozen winter. The icy weather was no obstacle to the 50 tough young men of the militia and the 200 Abenaki Indians. La Verendrye and his companions covered 300 miles through the forest in climatic conditions that would have killed the best troops of Europe. On February 28, they reached the outskirts of the village and lay concealed in the nearby pine forest for an entire night, shivering with cold for they dared not light a fire. Their rations were spent, and they had eaten nothing for the past twenty-four hours. They were so close to the village that they could savor the warm fragrance of the evening meal being cooked in the homes of the 300 inhabitants.

Deerfield was surrounded by a stout palisade. Three of its larger houses were designed for use as defense posts. They had a bullet-proof layer of bricks between the inner and outer wood sheathing of the walls. In two of the houses twenty English soldiers were billeted.

Two hours before dawn Pierre de la Verendrye and his companions removed their snowshoes and began to advance on the village across a three-foot-deep layer of frozen snow. The attack came as a complete and tragic surprise for the English. But the soldiers made the most of the fortified houses they were occupying. Aided by a number of men and women who had fled to them for shelter, they beat off one attack after another.

An hour after sunrise the French knew that the time had come to leave. Some of the Deerfield settlers had managed to escape in the darkness to the larger village of Hatfield, which lay a

few miles distant. Reinforcements from that village would be arriving soon. Loaded with salt
pork, smoked hams, flour, and bread, the French
and Indians began to depart. They took with
them eighty prisoners: men, women, and children.

The retreat began a little too late. The men of
Hatfield came after them, shot down a number
of Indians who had lagged behind, but were ambushed by the militia in the forest. Nine Frenchmen were killed in the raid, several were
wounded, and one was taken prisoner. The Indians lost forty-nine warriors; the English dead
amounted to fifty-two.

The French did their best to care for the
suffering prisoners during their long and exhausting retreat. In those awful weather conditions no
one could have done any more. But all the way
up the frozen Connecticut River between Ver-
mont and New Hampshire the captives kept les-
sening in numbers. Only forty of them returned
a few years later to Deerfield, where they reported that they had been well treated as workers and servants in French households.

The French detested Queen Anne's War as much as the British did. The settlers of both nations yearned to be left alone by the weary politicians and blundering kings of Europe, so that they could get on with building a new barn, planting spring crops, or splitting rails for a fence. La Verendrye was one of those settlers. Raiding sleeping villages to murder farmers and their families was not his idea of soldiering. Soon after his return to New France he went home to his family.

La Verendrye was now nineteen years old. He had grown during the past several years, but otherwise was much the same as when he paddled across the river to the militia headquarters in Montreal. During the expedition to Deerfield he had stood up well to the cold and hardships, earning the admiration of the older, more seasoned veterans with him. Thus, the French authorities did not let him enjoy a long vacation at the Isle Dupas. Less than a year later he was with the militia again. This time their mission was to descend the Saint Lawrence River in canoes and attack the English in Newfoundland. When the expedition set out, la Verendrye wore a thin gold stripe above the peak of his white cap to indicate his rank of ensign, or junior lieutenant.

A hundred militiamen reached the mouth of the river. They transferred to lumbering fishing boats, crewed by French fishermen, and sailed across the choppy Gulf of Saint Lawrence. The fleet landed at the little French settlement of Placentia on the west coast of Newfoundland's Avalon Peninsula. Then came a sixty-mile march across lonely and barren country to attack the English fort of Saint William, which guarded the settlement of Saint John's.

Apparently the English troops in the fort did not believe that this damp and unpleasant place could be of any great importance to England. They had given up guarding the harbor and the two batteries of guns that stood on opposite sides at its entrance. When the French approached the fort at three in the morning, the English were all soundly asleep in their blankets.

The militiamen were accompanied by ninety Indians. Another two or three hundred of the local French inhabitants had come along to share in the attack. Few of these settlers were armed with anything more deadly than old muskets loaded with duck shot.

Daniel Subercase, the militia leader, eyed the high, grass-grown walls of the fortress and thought about the ninety-two officers and men who comprised the garrison. To attack a fort of any kind would be a new experience for the militia. Even a stout wooden palisade was usually enough to discourage Indians. The local inhabitants were less interested in fighting than in plundering the fort.

Accordingly, Subercase declared prudently:

> Having shown the flag of France to these soldiers of England, we will leave them to cower and tremble behind their walls. But to reveal our invincible courage, we will use the guns at the harbor entrance to send a few iron shot whistling about their ears.

Everyone applauded this tactful decision. The militia trooped down to the harbor, turned the guns on the fort, and opened fire. Either their aim was bad or the walls of Fort Saint William were stronger than they looked. After three weeks of amusing themselves, the French became bored. They threw the guns into the harbor, packed up all the provisions they could carry, and began the long and uncomfortable journey back to Three Rivers.

Pierre de la Verendrye lost all interest in war for the time being. He resigned from the militia and began to look after his own career. The little station at La Gabelle gave him a start in the fur-trading business. A year later he was handling more furs and making a reasonable income.

After all the excitement during the past four years, the existence at Three Rivers seemed monotonous to la Verendrye. The settlers were interested only in their homes and families. For six months of the year, from October to March, the settlement generally lay deep in snow. The river was frozen, and overland travel was tiring and dangerous. The people did their best to amuse themselves at wedding feasts or baptisms, but they remained conscious all the while of the dark, frozen forest behind them and the great motionless expanse of river in front of them. For those six months, in fact, Three Rivers was isolated from the rest of the world.

A great longing for change gradually took possession of la Verendrye's mind. He longed to visit France, but travel of any kind was a costly business. For some time he thought over the problem. He was still thinking about it when he met Marie-Anne.

2
The Western Sea

Marie-Anne Dandonneau was the daughter of Louis Dandonneau, a Frenchman born in the New World. He had prospered quietly by purchasing likely sections of land up and down the Saint Lawrence River. He had a few rent-paying tenants, owned several houses, and was one of the more prosperous fur buyers. Already Dandonneau had transferred some of his property to Marie-Anne, and many young men in the settlements were eager to be on friendly terms with her and her family.

Pierre de la Verendrye, twenty-two years old, was the successful suitor. When Louis Dandonneau heard that Pierre and Marie-Anne wished to be married, he was approving but cautious.

"My daughter is only twelve years old," he said. "Although some girls marry at that age, I prefer to wait until she is older. In the meantime, I have no objection to your being betrothed."

Following the usual French custom, a formal contract of marriage was drawn up between Marie-Anne Dandonneau and Pierre Gaultier de la Verendrye. The document was dated November 9, 1707.

In the early spring of the following year la Verendrye paddled his canoe upstream to see his mother. Marie-Renée, his seventeen-year-old sister, was still at home, although planning soon to marry Christophe de la Jemeraye, a young man from Montreal in the fur trade. Louis was still in France with his regiment and in no hurry to return. Jean-Baptiste, an older brother, had become a priest.

La Verendrye went back to Three Rivers. He was still bored with life in the settlement and was

beginning to realize that the ordinary existence
of a small-time fur buyer was too monotonous
for him. The thought of spending another winter
in Three Rivers without a home of his own became depressing. Finally he made up his mind.

"I am going to France," he told his future
father-in-law and Marie-Anne. "The war there
may soon be over, but I think it will last long
enough for me to see Europe while I am serving
in the French Army."

Whatever Louis Dandonneau and Marie-
Anne thought privately of the idea they raised
no objection. The marriage would not take place
for at least another two years.

La Verendrye sailed from Quebec in the summer of 1708. Sixty-seven days later he was setting out to search for his brother's regiment in
France.

Young men from New France seldom had any
difficulty in entering the Army. The way of life
in their own country provided them with much
useful training. In field and camp they were han-
dier than most of the young French officers. La
Verendrye was given the rank of ensign. In a

smart uniform of blue and gold he marched off with his regiment to the battlefields of Europe.

Military life in Europe was very different from that of the militia in New France. European armies paid more attention to uniforms and ceremony than they did to the art of warfare. Soldiers were left to look after themselves when they camped in the field, and they were not taught how to make themselves comfortable or cook a meal. The officers traveled from place to place on horseback. Behind them came horse-drawn wagons containing tents, furniture, crates of foodstuffs, and personal luggage. Their cooks and servants rode with the wagons and took no part in the fighting.

At the battle of Malplaquet in France in September, 1709, la Verendrye and the Regiment of Brittany were part of the French Army that stood in shoulder-to-shoulder ranks to receive a charge by the English and Austrian cavalry. The battle that followed was so bloody that neither side could claim a victory. When the French finally withdrew, la Verendrye was left behind with a bullet wound in his chest and four saber slashes on his body.

He was luckier than most of the wounded men. There were few doctors and no medical orderlies in those primitive times. Several English soldiers ranging over the littered battlefield picked him up, carried him to a barn, and left him on a pile of straw. His wounds were dressed by nuns whose sympathy was greater than their medical knowledge. A local French doctor dug out the bullet and sewed up his other injuries. After this rough attention, he was left to live or die.

There were times during the next few weeks when la Verendrye nearly died. Only his wiry strength and tough constitution enabled him to survive. At the end of four months he was taken off to a prison camp. He remained in it for a year and then, for some military reason, was released. Only then did he discover that his elder brother, Louis, had been killed in the same battle.

La Verendrye was still weak and in no condition to resume his fighting career. The French

Army released him without delay. He left
Europe in 1711 and was back at Three Rivers
by the autumn.

Marie-Anne had believed for a year that he
was dead, but she had been awaiting definite
news.

"I have had enough of soldiering," la Verendrye told her. "I want independence now."

They were married on October 29, 1712.
Marie-Anne was seventeen years old and Pierre
twenty-seven.

Some months later Louis Dandonneau died.
Pierre and Marie-Anne went to live on the Isle
Dupas. They had a good, strong-walled house
surrounded with fifty acres of farming land.
Some of it was planted with wheat, and the rest
was used for the rearing of cattle and pigs. The
fur-trading post at La Gabelle remained under
the care of the manager who looked after the
place during la Verendrye's absence in France.

Life went smoothly for la Verendrye and his
wife. He operated the small farm, and during his
absences at La Gabelle or Three Rivers the place
was well run by his sturdy old mother and several

laborers. Marie-Anne spent her time looking after her young and increasing family.

Jean-Baptiste, la Verendrye's eldest son, was born in 1713. Then came Pierre in 1714, François in 1715, and Louis-Joseph in 1717. They were followed by two sisters, Marie-Anne born in 1721 and Marie-Catherine in 1724.

La Verendrye had only one grievance in his life at this time, but it continued to annoy him for years. Just before the battle of Malplaquet he had been promoted to the rank of first lieutenant. When he returned as an invalid to New France, his commission had been cancelled. Perhaps by way of consolation, the king had awarded him the rank of ensign in the French military forces stationed in New France. This lower rank entitled la Verendrye to draw a modest pension that was considerably less than it would have been for a lieutenant. La Verendrye believed that he should have been allowed to retain his lieutenancy as would have been customary for any officer with the citations for courage and devotion to duty that he had received while in the French Army.

The hard life led by the French-Canadian set-tlers, the isolation, and the loneliness of the long, dark winters caused many of them to develop some private complaint. Perhaps in a warmer and less hostile climate they would have forgotten whatever it was. In la Verendrye's case, this lost lieutenancy continued to rankle in his mind for years.

In 1724, thirteen years after he had returned to New France, la Verendrye decided to revisit France and submit a formal claim for the restoration of his lost rank. He applied to the governor of New France for the necessary permission to make the trip. The governor in turn inquired of the French authorities whether permission should be granted. All these formalities were an example of how closely the French government controlled those unfortunate Frenchmen who chose to live in New France.

At last the official reply came back:

> While permission is granted for Ensign Pierre de la Verendrye to visit France, we consider that he might be well advised to remain in New France

unless he has some particularly urgent reason for wishing to make the voyage.

The hint was clear to la Verendrye: he would do better to save the cost of the journey and forget about his lost lieutenancy. France was again at war with England, and as usual the country was almost bankrupt. Forty-year-old la Verendrye took the news badly. He became bored and restless in his home and eager for something new that would take his mind off his disappointment.

The governor-general of New France at that time was the Marquis Charles de Beauharnois. He was a tall, burly, practical man, who was making a success of his administration. A Navy officer for the greater part of his life, he was more interested than most of his predecessors in the unknown interior of New France. Although he was tied to his official duties in Quebec, he had an ardent interest in exploration. On the gray wall of his private study was a large-scale map of New France, which he knew to be very incomplete.

As far west as Lake Superior the map was reasonably correct. Beyond there were merely faint, uncertain lines and a great deal of blank space. Nothing was known of all that area. This ignorance on the part of the geographers continued to annoy Governor de Beauharnois every time his eyes lingered on the map.

By the Peace of Utrecht, which had ended Queen Anne's War in 1713, the Hudson Bay region was handed over to the English. France lost a rich fur-bearing area, which she had explored and developed, at least to a small extent, during the past fifty years. If only France could make some valuable discovery farther to the west, thought Beauharnois, it would compensate for the loss of Hudson Bay. One possibility was finding an easy route to the Western Sea, as the Pacific Ocean was called then. No one knew just how far to the west that sea lay. There were vague, uncertain rumors and legends among the Indian tribes that a great western bay or inlet or river—no one knew which—led into that ocean.

Beauharnois began to wonder if he could send a party to the shores of that bay. Then he would have access to the Pacific Ocean and from there to the wealthy coasts of China. If he could develop a new route to the wealth of the East Indies, France would grow enormously rich within a few years. Trade goods could be brought up the Saint Lawrence River to Montreal, sent through the passage provided by the Great Lakes, and then conveyed onward by some great unknown river or system of lakes to that saltwater inlet that leads to the Western Sea. From the mouth of the Saint Lawrence to the western end of Lake Superior was a distance of about 1500 miles. How much farther west a man would have to go to discover an inlet leading to the sea was shrouded in mystery.

Across the Atlantic Ocean, keen and eager minds in France were busy with the same problem. Even while Beauharnois was considering the problem beside the warm hearth in his office, a fresh communication reached him. The French Government was interested in the idea of a western inlet. Would His Excellency, the Marquis de Beauharnois, please ensure that a search for it was organized? Of course, due to difficult conditions in France, the work of exploration would have to be carried on without financial assistance from the Government.

While Pierre de la Verendrye was still living at his home in the Isle Dupas, Governor de Beauharnois sent out his first party of explorers. The leader was René Boucher de la Perrière, an uncle of la Verendrye, who took with him two Jesuit fathers named Guignas and Degonnor. They reached the southwestern shores of Lake Superior and hopefully built a fur-trading post beside Lake Pepin, which lay nearly 200 miles to the south.

The Fox Indians, who lived in that region, were no friends of the French nation, and they made their feelings clear. "We are glad that you have come to live so near us," they said to Boucher. "Our chief is planning to drive all the French out of New France. As you are the most westerly Frenchmen we know of, we can arrange for your scalping easily whenever our chief gives the word."

A year after they had been sent out by Beauharnois, Boucher and his companions were back in Quebec. Suddenly they had lost all enthusiasm for exploration. No one could blame them.

The governor began to wonder whom else to send. The population of New France was increasing slowly, but the total was not more than perhaps 50,000 settlers. The newer arrivals were unsuitable for life in the wild and had a great preference for living close to forts within the palisades of the settlements. Among the native-born French Canadians, the old spirit of adventure and discovery was wearing rather thin. There were plenty of *coureurs-de-bois*, or young woodsmen, who lived with the Indians, but they were an undisciplined and mostly illiterate class. Ordinary men preferred the security of their own acres and a warm fireside.

Pierre de la Verendrye's name suddenly occurred to the governor. There was a man, thought Beauharnois, who would make an admirable explorer. He was a trained soldier accustomed to hardship. He was Canadian-born and knew the forests. As a fur trader he had gained much useful experience with the Indians. Lastly, he was a man on whom one could rely absolutely, a man who was well established and would have money put by. The only difficulty was that la Verendrye probably would want a great deal of support before he would leave his own business.

Beauharnois invited la Verendrye to pay him a visit. In the privacy of the governor's office, he made his offer.

Lake Nipigon, to the north of Lake Superior, was in the heart of the fur-bearing country. The price offered in France for furs had been rising steadily ever since the Hudson Bay territory had passed into the hands of the English. A pioneer named du Lhut had spent a year or two near Lake Nipigon. He had reported favorably as to its suitability for a trading post. In fact, he had built his own outpost beside the Nipigon River. It had remained empty after du Lhut returned to the settlements, however, and was now probably in ruins.

"I want to expand our knowledge of the western territory of New France," the governor told la Verendrye. "France must make a search for some navigable inlet that leads perhaps to the Western Sea. No man knows how far to the west that supposed inlet may lie, but I am sure that a man cannot go there direct from our settlements here on the Saint Lawrence. The journey will have to be made in a series of steps. Each step will be marked by a trading post."

Beauharnois continued to explain his scheme. The first post would be built somewhere in the area of Lake Nipigon. The next one would be some 250 miles farther on, at the western end of Lake Superior. Still another would be located in territory probably totally unknown to the French.

"Each post must support itself," said Beauharnois. "I fear that France, while most anxious to find this route to the west, is unable or unwilling to provide any funds for exploration. The fur posts themselves will have to pay the whole cost of the venture for there is little indeed that my government in New France can do to help. There are times when I despair the lack of foresight shown in France, but no matter. Monsieur de la Verendrye, I offer you the post of Nipigon and the command of all others that will be built during the next few years. I promise you the sole fur concession for all that vast area. No other Frenchman will have the right to enter any part of your region and trade in furs on his own account, except with your approval. But you, in turn, must try to expand to the westward as swiftly as you can and to carry out what exploration becomes possible with the profits earned by this new development of the fur trade."

The offer was very tempting. Many Frenchmen would have accepted it and thanked their good fortune for the opportunity to do so. But la Verendrye in those days was not the type to rush into an agreement. For a full two weeks he remained in Quebec, and during that time he continued to meet the governor almost daily. They studied maps of North America, sought in vain for even scanty information regarding the unknown western coast of New France, and discussed probable profits and costs. While the wages, trade goods, and supplies that would make up the costs could be estimated, the profits were impossible to reckon. How many bales of furs were the Indians taking northward yearly to the English trading posts in Hudson Bay? How

many of those Indians could be tempted to trade
with the French instead? What was the total possible fur production of the vast area? The whole
scheme proposed by Beauharnois began to appear
as a vast and exciting gamble. A man might stand
to gain an almost incredible fortune; he might
also end up with nothing.

La Verendrye made up his mind at last. With
the money he had saved and the credit he could
obtain, he would be able to make a start. "France
and you, Sire," he said, "are willing to issue a
license that will provide a man with the chance
to gain great wealth for himself or to end up pen-
niless. Whichever way the wheel of fortune may
turn, he must first pay, and pay heavily, for permission to gamble. Even so, I accept your offer,
Sire."

Beauharnois smiled. "Neatly put, I may say. I
am delighted that you are prepared to gamble. I
could have found no better man in all New
France. Younger and less responsible men, yes.
Mature and experienced veterans like yourself,
no."

Neither then nor at any later time did la Verendrye express regret at leaving his comfortable home in the Isle Dupas. During the years he had lived with Marie-Anne and their children he had developed it efficiently. Now there was a barn, good timbered sheds for the cattle, and fifty acres of well-fenced fields bearing crops that grew profitably in the rich black soil. The house itself showed evidence of the modest prosperity that la Verendrye had acquired. It had solid stone walls and a new shingled roof. In the stone-floored kitchen were copper kettles and cooking pots that had come all the way from France. There were feather mattresses and ponderous wooden chests full of blankets and linen. A deep, chill cellar kept meat fresh even during the summer months. There was a small mirror, which was a rarity, on the wall of the principal bedroom and another in the sitting room. Except for the kitchen, the floors were made of smoothly adzed pine logs.

Living in this house in the year of 1726 were Marie-Anne and the children: thirteen-year-old Jean-Baptiste, twelve-year-old Pierre, eleven-year-old François, nine-year-old Louis-Joseph,

five-year-old Marie-Anne, and two-year-old
Marie-Catherine. The la Verendryes had a well-
run home in which security and contentment
existed. Still, forty-one-year-old Pierre de la
Verendrye was prepared to leave it.

Perhaps he remembered the excitement and
dangers of his earlier years. He may have re-
sented the thought of growing old in a safe but
monotonous existence beside the river. But no
one can say for sure what were the reasons that
tempted him to launch out in a new venture and
to gamble everything that he had gained over the
years.

Marie-Anne soon knew that her husband had
made up his mind and that nothing could cause
him to alter it. She was a quiet, self-reliant, and
capable woman, who busied herself with the
home and seldom interfered in her husband's
affairs. "Our elder boys can help the *engagés*
(hired workers) to run the farm," she said. "This
house is our own, and we are well provided for.
The manager you have at La Gabelle knows me,
and I have no doubt that he can be trusted to send
me his accounts from time to time. We will be

able to manage very well. But I think I will take the children to Montreal during the winter, where we will be safer from the Indians. In the spring and summer we will remain here on the farm."

The fur trade was centered in Montreal. La Verendrye was able to make daily trips across the river, discuss his business with the merchants, and return to his home in the evening. By that time the news of his fur monopoly had become known throughout the settlements. The merchants were eager and willing to do business with him. Anything he wanted in the way of supplies they would be glad to provide, whether he paid now or later. They suggested that the cost of what he bought could be deducted from the money earned by his first consignments of furs to reach Montreal.

The plans appeared safe and simple in those warm and sturdy trading stores. In fact, the whole undertaking was bigger than anything la Verendrye had handled previously. His little business at La Gabelle was nothing compared with this present venture. When he spent the money that he had available, he did not hesitate to obtain the further necessary goods on credit. He also raised a few hundred dollars in extra cash by signing more papers.

La Verendrye ended up with a handy cargo of trade goods, three new canoes, and six *voyageurs*. These French-Canadian rivermen were powerful fellows, who could wield a paddle all day, carry enormous loads for long distances at portages, and had a great liking for their strenuous and lonely life. They worked hard and played hard. Most of them were dead at forty, worn out by their labors. However, there were always plenty of other young men available to fill the places of those who disappeared. New France had no industries to provide employment, and new recruits were almost invariably those who were bored with life on the farms where they had been raised.

On the early morning of a June day in the year 1727, la Verendrye left his home on the Isle Dupas and walked down to the awaiting canoes. He had put aside the burdensome clothing worn by the wealthier menfolk of the settlements. Instead he was dressed much as the militiaman he had been twenty years ago. He wore a deerskin jacket and knee breeches, heavy woolen stockings, and soft Indian moccasins. On his back was a leather knapsack containing a few necessary items, topped off by a rolled blanket. A hunting knife was on his belt and a musket on his shoulder.

When he left Montreal that morning, la Verendrye was older than most of the men who ventured into the wilds. His shoulder-length hair and beard already were touched with gray. At forty-two, when others of the same age were beginning to take life a little more easily, he was setting forth on an entirely new and unknown career.

3
The First Outpost

Past forests draped with grapevine and waters alive with wildfowl, la Verendrye and his six canoe men paddled during those summer months. When they steered toward the nearest shore at sunset they sometimes met parties of friendly Indians, who loaded them with gifts of maize and fish. These Hurons questioned la Verendrye as to the reason for his journey and his destination.

"I am going to set up a trading post farther to the west, on Lake Nipigon," he replied.

"Do not pass out of our country," the Indians replied. "If you go too far, you will come to the region inhabited by the Sioux. They are a warlike and dangerous tribe, as bad perhaps as those Iroquois living south of the Saint Lawrence."

"And what lies beyond the land of these Sioux of whom you speak?" asked la Verendrye.

The Indians looked doubtful. "We have not been there. The tribes say different things. We have heard that tribes of fish eaters live beyond the Sioux. In their country white men like yourselves ride horses and wear suits of armor. But do not try to go there. Stay at Lake Nipigon. The Crees who dwell in that area are our blood relations. You will have no trouble with them."

La Verendrye was hearing the legend that most of the Indians related in one form or another. Although they were invariably vague as to the exact direction, they spoke of "a great body of water," which might mean the sea. "Tell me what you know of the Western Sea," said la Verendrye. "I do not intend to go there on this journey, but I am interested to learn more of the white men who you say inhabit its shores."

The Indians became more vague. They had heard this and been told that. They did not know how many marches would be necessary in order to reach the great water. Their lives were spent in their own tribal area, where they grew their crops and sold what furs they obtained to the Frenchmen.

Three months after he had left Montreal la Verendrye reached the Nipigon River. The old trading post, or Fort Sainte Anne as it had been named, stood in a small grassy clearing some fifty yards from the bank of the stream. Pine trees grew luxuriantly on the low hills in the distance, but their somber, monotonous green was blended with the brighter autumn shades of walnut, pine, and black-tufted ash. Between the moss-covered walls of the cabin and the water's edge was a low-lying meadow dotted with swamp maple and golden-hued birch trees. Half a mile farther upstream some Cree Indians lived in a small village of birch-bark tents. Their fields of maize, pumpkins, and sunflowers, from which they made hair oil, were ripening in the sun.

Old du Lhut had made his buildings solidly.

The post had been built in 1670, but nearly sixty years later the timber walls of the living quarters and the adjacent fur store were still serviceable. However, the adzed wooden doors had been removed by the Indians for firewood, and the bark roofs had collapsed. Some wild raspberry bushes had taken root in the beaten earth floor of one cabin, and their thorny branches projected from the empty window. Even so, the original structures were usable, and la Verendrye's *voyageurs* set about repairing them without delay. The threat of approaching winter made them work quickly.

The Crees, like their blood relations the Nipissings, were an unusually superstitious tribe, who believed themselves to be continually beset by demons and mischievous spirits. They came trooping from their huts to welcome the Frenchmen and uttered delighted exclamations when they learned that la Verendrye intended to spend the winter in their midst. While their womenfolk gathered berries for the winter stores, the Indians helped with the rebuilding of the cabins and did their best to answer questions.

"This river is full of fish," they said. "The forests abound with deer and bear. Often there are moose. We will supply you with corn and eels as well as with furs. Perhaps in return you will come hunting with us, for your muskets will provide plenty of fresh meat. We know that a gun can kill at longer range than a bow and arrow."

While autumn faded and the first snows of winter began to flutter across the landscape, la Verendrye held many conversations with these friendly Indians. Once again he sought knowledge about the Western Sea, and once again the Crees were understandably vague. They did not know what an ocean was; it was something beyond their imagination. Farther north, so la Verendrye had heard, there were tribes who referred to Hudson Bay as the Stinking Water, but these Nipigon River Indians were ignorant of the name. All they knew was the same legend told by the other tribes.

"Yes, we have heard of a great body of water," they declared. "It lies many marches to the west. No, we do not know how to reach it. The Sioux

are our enemies. The water lies beyond the frontiers of their country. Yes, we have heard of
white men who live in great stone houses and
ride on the backs of those animals they call
horses."

La Verendrye was fascinated by this recurring
story of white men and a far-off body of water.
At the same time he was never sure of its ac-
curacy. Did the supposed bay really lie to the
west or were the Indians referring to the Frenchmen living at the mouth of the Mississippi or
perhaps the Spanish colonies on the shores of the
Gulf of Mexico? They were ignorant of the compass, and possibly they might be confusing west
with southwest or even with south.

The dark months of winter passed in reasonable comfort. Both Indians and Frenchmen remained well fed. Game was not difficult to find,
and the Crees had stored plentiful reserves of
food. The yield of furs was disappointingly small.
however, perhaps because this tribe had not developed a strong liking for European trade goods.
As the days lengthened, la Verendrye eyed his
almost empty fur store. Two bales of beaver, one

of marten, and three of fox represented the total
that they had gathered. The sale of these furs
would not fetch enough money to reimburse the
merchants for the money and trade goods they
had supplied.

La Verendrye was not as worried as perhaps
he should have been. His outlook was changing.
Whereas in former times the collection of furs
had figured largely in his life, the discovery of
the Western Sea now occupied most of his
thoughts. In that warm but lonely hut in the middle of nowhere, he had found freedom to live as
he chose. Bills and receipts and invoices were fad-
ing into the background of his mind. La Verendrye was being transformed into an explorer
unknowingly.

In the spring of 1728, he set off with one companion for Montreal and Quebec. The governor
would be awaiting his first reports on the progress he had made.

Somewhere on the Great Lakes they sighted
another canoe. In it was Father Degonnor, who
earlier had gone with Perrière to Lake Pepin. A
big, powerful man whom the Indians had nick-

named Saranhès—the big tree—he, too, had spent the winter in the wilds. Only a man of his tremendous constitution and determination could have survived the primitive conditions that he had been living in. Although Father Degonnor had chosen to become a Jesuit missionary, he was an explorer at heart. During the winter he had spent much time learning what he could of the unknown regions that lay to the west. Now he was returning to Montreal, accompanied by several Indians, to report on the results of his trip.

This meeting caused la Verendrye to change his plans.

"Let us camp for a day or two so that you can write a report," Degonnor suggested. "I will carry it to Montreal and see that it is sent on to Governor Beauharnois."

The report was prepared and sealed. It was placed, together with the bales of fur, in Degonnor's canoe. La Verendrye hastened back immediately to the Nipigon River. There was so much to do, so many plans to prepare, that he had lost all interest in revisiting the settlements. Before this summer ended, he hoped to establish a second trading post, which would lie still farther toward the unknown west.

A surprise awaited him at Fort Sainte Anne. Somewhere along the way they had passed unknowingly a convoy of three large canoes carrying sixteen men and a heavy cargo of merchandise. The whole expedition had been arranged by Marie-Anne. She had persuaded the Montreal merchants to grant an extension of her husband's credit and had hired the men who manned the canoes, picking them with much care and experience. They had been placed under the command of a young man named Jean-Baptiste de Verchères, who came from one of the leading families in New France.

Jean-Baptiste had brought with him a letter from Beauharnois. The governor, who was an honorable man, had not gone back on his word, but in tactful language he made an unexpected alteration in the original agreement between himself and la Verendrye. He said in so many words:

As your present trading post at Forte Sainte Anne is well known, it can hardly be regarded as one of the new line of westward-running forts which I have entrusted you to build. I have no doubt that the farther west you progress, the greater will become the yield of furs and thus, one hopes, the greater profit to yourself. I suggest therefore that young Verchères take over Fort Sainte Anne and run it as his own. This will leave you free to develop your new posts. Verchères will be responsible for his own supply of trade goods and the disposal of the pelts he obtains.

It was too late that year for la Verendrye to undertake the proposed move. He and his six *voyageurs* shared the living quarters with the men whom Verchères had brought. Another hut to provide additional accommodation was built and finished before the autumn began. Now that la Verendrye was no longer responsible for the trade in furs at this post, he was able to spend more time searching for fresh information. That winter he met a valuable informant.

The man was a Cree chief named Tacchigis. He was an unusually venturesome Indian, who had wandered from place to place in his younger years and was full of stories. He spoke of a great

river running strongly to the west and of two
others that flowed south. He had heard of white
men in armor, but had never seen a horse. Yes,
these white men may have lived in a direction
that was more southerly than toward the true
west. No, they were not the Frenchmen who
lived at the mouth of the Mississippi. He knew of
that river. These other white men lived far, far
to the west. He had heard that long ago, before
even his own grandfather was born, some Indians
from the west declared that they had seen "a
vast white canoe with towering white wings"
sailing into a bay that was situated to the west.
Yes, the country was toward the setting sun, declared Tacchigis emphatically, beyond the land
of the Sioux. Choosing a time when the Sioux
were at peace with their neighbors, this party of
Indians later had returned to their own tribe,
who, he believed, were named the Mandans. But
once again Tacchigis, not having made the journey himself, had no idea how many marches
would be needed to reach the place where the
big white sailing ship was said to have been seen.

With all this fresh mixture of legend and

doubtful information in his mind, la Verendrye set off with his *voyageurs* for Quebec. There were matters he wished to discuss with Beauharnois, he wanted to pay a visit, however brief, to his wife and family, and he had decided that he must visit the merchants to whom he owed money.

The governor listened closely to everything that la Verendrye told him. "This is interesting," he said. "I may tell you that when Father Degonnor delivered your reports and maps to me, I asked Gaspard de Léry, my esteemed civil engineer to examine them. He came to the conclusion that some westward flowing river might possibly discharge into the vast bay said to have been discovered by an Englishman named Sir Francis Drake about a hundred and fifty years ago. How far to the west that bay lies, we have no way of telling. Still, de Léry supports your ideas and theories. So do I, for that matter. But in the report you sent me, you suggested that from some lake the Indians call Ouinipigon (Winnipeg) only ten marches would be needed. This morning you suggest that the distance might be greater. How much greater do you think?"

La Verendrye hesitated before making his reply. "At the time of my first report I had not seen for myself the great westward distances of this continent. I still have not seen much. But now, whenever I cross great lakes and ascend rivers that seem to run on endlessly, my ideas of vastness continue to grow. This land seems to stretch westward forever. Ten marches, I said? Then, Sire, I say to you now that I might as well have written twenty marches."

Beauharnois nodded thoughtfully. "Bearing in mind what you have said, we must prepare to stretch our trading posts even farther to the west than we originally planned. I propose that a fort at Rainy Lake should be your next move, but of course the Minister of Marine and Colonies in France will have to approve of the plan. I do not think that he will disappoint us, but I doubt that he will try to arrange a government grant for your exploration either. One suspects that the honorable ministers believe that the nearer to

Paris all money is kept, the more carefully they can supervise its spending."

Jean-Frédéric, the Comte de Maurepas, Minister of Marine and Colonies, was an overprivileged young nobleman at the French court. His high position indicated what could be achieved in those times if one were fortunate enough to be born into the right family. As a boy of fourteen he had succeeded his father as minister. The actual duties of his position were fulfilled by another nobleman whose daughter he was destined to marry in a few year's time. Maurepas took over full responsibility for his post at the age of twenty-four. He was now twenty-nine and generally regarded as a young man with a quick and clever mind. Several days after holding a conversation he could repeat, almost word for word, everything that had been said.. He never forgot names or dates or similar details, and he certainly never forgot his dazzling social duties.

In his ornate mansion in Paris, waited on hand and foot, enjoying infinitely more wealth than was good for him, young Maurepas found life in the wilds of Canada difficult to visualize. Explorers to him were rather impossible people who were always wanting to go to some place not marked on the map. Such places always had peculiar names that were impossible for civilized Frenchmen to pronounce. Although these explorers seemed to live in a very barbaric fashion, sometimes even among savages with whom they shared the most extraordinary foods, they always wanted money. Sometimes these tiresome fellows actually got themselves killed by the barbarians.

Governor-General Beauharnois, as Comte de Maurepas read in the latest report from New France, now requested permission for la Verendrye to establish a trading post at a location called Rainy Lake as a further step on his journey of exploration to find the Western Sea. The most agreeable fact about the request was that the proposed trip could be made without expense to the French Government. Only a reasonabe sum to buy presents for the Indians was needed. The amount was the equivalent of $1500 in modern currency.

Maurepas wondered irritably why all these plans were necessary. Why couldn't la Verendrye simply pick up a musket and a cooking pot, put a blanket on his back, and walk off to the west to find the Western Sea? If he kept going far enough, he would be sure to reach the coast. This present way of building trading posts looked as if it would take years. Perhaps la Verendrye was more interested in acquiring wealth from furs and was merely using exploration as a pretext to obtain for himself the richest fur-bearing regions.

Feeling rather peevish about the whole matter, Maurepas consulted Father Charlevoix, a missionary recently returned from New France. Charlevoix was an enthusiastic amateur explorer who had traveled the basin of the Great Lakes and knew his way around most of that region. He spoke highly of la Verendrye and reassured Maurepas that the financial request was reasonable.

At last Maurepas made up his mind. His reply to the governor's request reached Quebec in the spring of 1731. Permission was granted for the new post at Rainy Lake. The sum of $1000, but not $1500, could be spent on the purchase of gifts. The administration at Quebec would have to foot the bill.

La Verendrye was at his home on the Isle Dupas when this news reached him.

"It seems that you are trying to explore the whole of New France on your own," Marie-Anne said to him. "You are expected to pay your own way, France gives you little money to buy trade goods, and yet Comte de Maurepas continually urges you to make haste to find this bay leading to the Western Sea."

"The trading post I am going to establish near Rainy Lake will be in an area rich in marten and beaver," replied la Verendrye. "Even though I am short of everything, I still hope to obtain enough pelts to restore the merchants' confidence in myself."

"We are not short of debts," replied Marie-Anne. "They seem to be increasing all the time. Our older boys want to accompany you when you set off again. Let them come with you. They will be of great help, and perhaps your business affairs will improve."

Jean-Baptiste, la Verendrye's eldest son, was

eighteen years old. Taller and heavier than his father, he was shrewd, hard-working, and light-hearted. Pierre, the second son, was aged seventeen. He was short and stocky, like la Verendrye himself, more serious than Jean-Baptiste, and inclined to be taciturn. François, who was only sixteen, was short, dark, and heavily built. Slow in his thoughts and movements, inclined to make a muddle of most things he tackled, François perhaps should have been left behind.

Louis-Joseph, the fourth and brightest boy, was only fourteen. Some of the family relatives were going to find a place for him in their business. He was unusually quick with figures and had much aptitude for learning. But Louis-Joseph was not interested in an office and a high stool. He longed to set off in a canoe with his father and brothers and share their adventures. Marie-Anne, however, remained firm. For another year or so Louis-Joseph must continue to go to school.

4
The New Recruits

One more valuable recruit was still to join la Verendrye. Christophe de la Jemeraye, his nephew, was a young man of twenty-three. Already he had lived an adventurous existence in the wilds. This tall, rangy young man was almost as dark in complexion as any Indian. His blue eyes contrasted strikingly with his swarthy features and long black hair. At sixteen he had joined the local militia and served for several years. Only recently he and another daring young man, one who spent most of his time living as a *coureur-de-bois*, had returned from a winter stay in a Sioux camp somewhere near the headwaters of the Mississippi River. Jemeraye was still wearing the handsomely embroidered leather tunic and mocassins made by the Sioux women. He was as valuable an assistant as could be obtained anywhere in New France. La Verendrye offered him the position of second-in-command and la Jemeraye accepted.

"The trip will be a chance to learn something about the fur trade and to go on living in the wilderness," he said. "I could not take to farming or to life in a merchant house."

La Verendrye's standing in the community was so high that he was able to obtain fresh credit from the Montreal traders. On this occasion, however, he had to arrange for his militia pension to be collected by a merchant, Claude Bruyère, to whom he owed the most money. Clearly there was no quick fortune to be earned in the fur trade. The furs were obtainable from the Indians, but wages, supplies, and the cost of freightage by canoe over enormous distances were eating up profits at an alarming rate. Perhaps the new post at Rainy Lake would bring about an improvement in the financial position.

Early in June, 1731, la Verendrye's men completed the loading of six thirty-five-foot canoes, which lay alongside the wharf at Montreal. Fifty *voyageurs* were to form the crews, eight or nine of them to a boat. These birchbark canoes were only four feet in width and light enough to be easily handled at the roughest portage. Yet the strength of their cedar frames enabled each one to carry a total weight, including crew and cargo, of nearly four tons.

The imminent departure of la Verendrye's party caused much gossip in the settlement. Nearly everyone was aware that a chain of trading posts was gradually being extended toward the west. It was known that from the last of these posts la Verendrye would set out one day to try to discover a navigable river or bay that led to the Western Sea. Although the settlers had lost most of their interest in exploration, they realized that such a discovery would be of the greatest importance to New France. There were optimists in Montreal who even prophesied that before long their settlement would be astride a new and prosperous trade route to the Spice Islands and China.

At the Lachine Rapids, a wide, ugly, and dangerous stretch of rushing water nine miles above Montreal, the first portage had to be made. The canoes then headed into the Ottawa River, which was the usual and quickest route to the western Great Lakes.

This river was no longer as safe as it once had been. Seventy-two years earlier the friendly Hurons who lived along its banks had been almost wiped out by the Iroquois. Those who survived this massacre fled in fear and horror to the west, where they found refuge in the country to the north of Lake Superior. Ever since that massacre, French canoes using the river had to be constantly on guard against attack by roving parties of Iroquois. These war parties were growing more and more dangerous since their friends and allies, the English, had taken to providing them with good muskets and generous quantities of powder and lead.

Across Lake Nipissing and into French River

la Verendrye led his party. The canoes glided in
the deep stillness past little islets on which isolated
pines stood straight and dark. The route led onward close to sun-scorched rocky crags, where
the air quivered in the heat and mosses were
crisped brown by the sun. Eighty miles down-
river the shores widened out, the water lilies
were left behind, and the canoes glided onto the
waters of Lake Huron. Soon they came to the
Jesuit mission and the well-run French trading
post at Michilimackinac that had been established
there for the past six or seven years. The place
stood on the south side of the strait between
Lakes Huron and Michigan, only a few miles
from the modern Mackinaw City. La Verendrye
and his party paused for a day at this spot to catch
great quantities of whitefish.

The three la Verendrye boys were utterly ab-
sorbed in everything they saw. They gazed
wonderingly at the almost unending forest of
walnut, chestnut, and wild plum trees. They
watched herds of deer roaming in the woods.
Feeding turkeys clucked and gobbled, and from
time to time great flocks of swans, white and

gleaming against the bright sky, passed overhead.

The time spent at Michilimackinac became two and then three days. During the long journey from the settlements, la Verendrye had been thinking about this new expedition and the prospects ahead. For the first time, it seemed, he began to have misgivings. The farther he traveled from Montreal, the larger became the debts he was incurring. Would he be able to collect enough bales of fur during the coming winter to liquidate them? How would he be able to run his trading posts during the lengthy period that he would be searching for the Western Sea? La Jemeraye must accompany him on that journey; the young man was invaluable in his ability to establish friendly terms with the new tribes that they might meet. Jean-Baptiste, the eldest son, probably would become a good manager in a few years' time, but the boy would have to be older before he could accept such responsibility. Another three years perhaps? Would Maurepas be prepared to wait that long or would he lose patience and forbid all further expansion toward the west?

La Verendrye composed a letter to Maurepas while staying at Michilimackinac and sent a copy of it to Governor-General Beauharnois.

> Our voyage to the present has been successful and without incident. I have high hopes that before this summer ends, our new post will be built at Rainy Lake and that we will acquire great quantities of excellent furs. But it is of another matter, Sire, of which I wish to speak now. Although I hold myself at your disposal to make an earnest effort to discover the Western Sea, of which we have heard so much from the Indians, at least a half of which may be true, the debts I have incurred on the past and present expeditions I have led continue to be a great burden to me. If you, Sire, will see fit to do me the great honor of extending to five years my present monopoly of furs in the Rainy Lake region, then I will be able to recover the money I have spent. Otherwise I do not know how I may come out of the present affair with a modest profit to myself.

Although la Verendrye had faith in Governor-General Beauharnois's promise of a monopoly of the fur trade in the regions to be explored, he did not have similar confidence in the minister. He was worried lest Maurepas, losing interest and patience, might override the governor's promise and open up those areas to others. La Verendrye would be swept aside and left to find his own way out of debt as best he could.

The letter was left at Michilimackinac to be taken to the settlements by the first canoe to depart. La Verendrye's own flotilla set off again. Knowing how quickly a disastrous storm could arise on Lake Superior, he took care to lead his canoes along the northern shore without losing sight of land. The lake was left behind when they swung north into Pigeon River and began to cross the chain of smaller lakes that forms its course.

La Verendrye and la Jemeraye chose the site of the trading post at a spot where Rainy Lake finds its outlet in the river that bears the same name. There, in the middle of a three-acre grove of fine oak trees, the fort was built. It consisted of two main houses, each containing two spacious rooms equipped with wide stone fireplaces and outside chimneys. These fireplaces were so large that a whole deer could be roasted in them.

The post was surrounded with a double palisade of wooden posts thirteen feet high. Young la
Jemeraye was insistent that this palisade should
be built. He pointed out that Sioux war parties
had been known to come as far as Rainy Lake
and they would be deterred only by strong de-
fenses. A special stone-walled storehouse—perhaps to be used as an emergency fortification—
stood a little distance from the living quarters. It
contained the trade goods and gunpowder bar-
rels. To the fort itself was given the name of Fort
Saint Pierre.

Some of the *engagés* soon began to make trouble. Back in the early summer in Montreal, the
prospect of a trip to the Great Lakes and regular
wages had appealed to them. Now, in this isolated spot with none of their own kind within
several hundred miles, they began to change their
minds. They became bored and were always
afraid of a sudden Indian attack. The thought of
spending a winter in the trading post, when the
cold would be bitter, the nights long, and the
food monotonous, increased their ill humor.

"We did not realize how far from civilization

we would be," they said. "Nor did we know that we might be exposed to Indian war parties. That was not mentioned in our contracts."

"Best let them go," la Jemeraye advised la Verendrye. "Men like them will never be of any use to us when we build other posts even more distant from their beloved settlements. The sooner they get back to them, the better we all shall be!"

La Verendrye allowed thirty of them to depart in three canoes. He warned them, however, that the season was late for such a long journey and that they would be wiser to remain in the trading post for the winter. The *engagés* refused to listen to him and scampered off in a great hurry, being anxious to reach Montreal before the rivers froze.

They were not as careful on Lake Superior as la Verendrye had been and traveled straight across it. Far out in the middle of the lake they were overtaken by a storm. They headed for a distant island, but by the time they reached it, their stores were soaked and the canoes half-swamped. The men crawled ashore miserably,

managed to get a fire going, and sat around it for
the next three days, closely wrapped in blankets.
During all this time driving sleet and a gale-force
wind prevented them from cooking anything.
They were forced to exist on soggy scraps of
food. The *engagés* finally reached the Saint Lawrence after a trip that was worse than anything
they ever had visualized, much worse than a
winter would have been at Rainy Lake.

Parties of Cree and Assiniboin Indians came
to Fort Saint Pierre during the winter. From
these visitors la Verendrye learned that a third
tribe in the district, the Monsonis, were planning
to attack the Sioux as soon as spring returned.

"They must be stopped," la Verendrye said to
la Jemeraye. "If this region goes up in the flames
of tribal war, there'll be no furs and no exploration."

Both men did everything they could to keep
the tribes at peace. Still, the war fever began to
spread among the Crees and the Assiniboins. Apparently they would unite with the Monsonis
against the Sioux. Already the Indians were ne-

glecting their fur trapping noticeably. They were spending most of their time binding arrowheads onto shafts, making new bows, and recalling stories of ancient victories.

During those long winter nights while he lay in his bunk and watched the glowing fire, la Verendrye continued to think about his financial position. The small quantities of furs he had collected were only a fraction of what he had hoped for. It was doubtful if they would fetch enough to cover his payroll. His total debts amounted to some $8,000, a formidable sum in those days.

The temptation came to him to abandon his plans for the future. Perhaps he should cancel everything to save himself from the financial swamp into which he was sinking. If he gave up all ideas of exploration financed by the profits from fur trading, he could return to his home at Isle Dupas. By one means or another he would be able to pay his outstanding debts. Let Maurepas and the governor-general find someone else to do their exploring for them!

La Verendrye soon abandoned these thoughts. This vast country of lake and forest and prairie had gained too strong a hold on him. He was too attracted by the dream of finding an estuary that ran to the west coast. Supposing, just supposing, a navigable river leading to it lay only a few hundred miles more to the west. How would he forgive himself if he gave up his search when on the verge of a discovery that might result in a great new trade route?

By the time the sun grew warmer and the days longer, la Verendrye had made up his mind. Even though he was suffering adversity at present, he would not throw away his onward progress to the west. If that inlet existed, then he intended to find it.

5
The Impatient Tribes

By May in that year of 1732, a few more bales of fur had been collected. Nineteen-year-old Jean-Baptiste was put in command of two canoes laden with the furs and told to take them to the trading post at Michilimackinac, where he would be able to send them to Montreal.

As soon as the canoes had left, la Verendrye began to plan another fort still farther to the west. The new post he had in mind was at Lake of the Woods, a distance of more than 100 miles. He had noticed that Rainy River flowed toward the northwest in the direction of Lake of the Woods. Was it possible, he wondered, that already he was nearing the headwaters of some mighty and unknown river that flowed toward the Western Sea?

Lake of the Woods was about fifty miles long; its width varied from fifty miles to less than half of that distance. It was the most beautiful stretch of water that la Verendrye had seen. To the north, its surface was covered with grassy and fertile little islands. On those islands and across the countryside as far as the eye could see grew unending forests of pine, fir, and oak. Deer were abundant, and the soil was deep, dark, and rich.

La Jemeraye was delighted with this new site. "We may be short of money and trade goods," he said, "but we are richer than most men in the things that really count. The plum trees will provide us with all the fruit we need. This good earth will grow corn and other crops. With a little money for necessities a man could live here all his days and be content."

The spot they chose for the new fort was on a small, tree-covered headland on the western side of Lake of the Woods, within the present-day State of Minnesota. There the men built a rectangular stockade of fifteen-foot posts, measuring one hundred feet long and sixty feet wide. Inside this defense stood four roomy log-walled cabins for the *voyageurs*, a smaller cabin for la Verendrye and his sons, a powder magazine, and a storehouse. The new post was completed in September. It was named Fort Saint Charles.

La Verendrye's enthusiasm was returning. He forgot his gloomy thoughts of the winter months. The local Indians told him that at the northern end of Lake of the Woods lay another and larger river, which also ran to the west. This river, known now as the Winnipeg, was supposed to flow into another large lake. From that lake still another river—the modern Assiniboine—also ran to the west. La Verendrye thought that possibly he was nearer to the Western Sea than he had believed. In that case, the day might come when this new fort would be an important staging point on the route toward it.

During that autumn la Verendrye worked from morning to night. He put Fort Saint Pierre at Rainy Lake in the care of la Jemeraye. The young man went back there in order to supervise preparations for another winter. Jean-Baptiste returned from Michilimackinac, bringing with him supplies and a limited stock of trade goods. Luckily he had met at Michilimackinac the agent of one of the Montreal traders to whom la Verendrye owed money. This man had taken charge of the furs and advanced a certain amount of money on them, so Jean-Baptiste was able to buy goods right away. La Verendrye made a trip back to Rainy Lake, supervised the division of the stores between Fort Saint Charles and Fort Saint Pierre, and put the men to work. He kept them busy planting rice and vegetables and had them pick and dry the plums that would be a necessary part of their diet when winter came. Thus, the summer season of 1732 went past with nothing done in the way of exploration.

The winter of 1732 arrived. La Verendrye and his men remained warm and well-fed at both forts. The local Indians were still in a state of peace; they had been dissuaded, thanks to la Verendrye's earlier efforts, from marching against the Sioux. Now they began to bring in more furs than they had collected during the previous winter. As the bales increased in the storehouse at Fort Saint Charles, la Verendrye became more cheerful. Never previously had he been able to gather so many furs during a winter. If only he could persuade the Indians to remain at peace, his fortunes would improve. Before long he might be able to reduce his debts.

In the spring of 1733 la Verendrye called a meeting of the Cree chiefs. They came with their families and attendants, erecting their tents and lighting their campfires close to the stockade. An Indian village of almost 300 people appeared from nowhere within a couple of days.

La Verendrye then proceeded to address them:

I ask you not to make war against the Sioux. It is not only my wish but that of the White Father in Quebec. Before long I hope to set off on a journey to the west, and such a journey is possible only in times of peace. How can I go into the Sioux country when that tribe, knowing that the Crees are friends, may consider me an enemy? I have no wish to leave my scalp, and those of my companions, dangling from their tent poles. I have seen wars, my friends, not only in this country but in my own. Wars bring bitterness and sorrow and hatred. Seldom do they produce any good. Let us live together in peace, let us lie down at night by our own firesides for as long as the Sioux may decide to leave us alone.

The leading chief among the Crees stood up to reply. He was a short, broad-shouldered man of about forty-five, and his name was Mah-to-he-ha, the Old Bear. His headdress, made of raccoon skins, was ornamented with buffalo horns, and he wore an unusually fine ermine robe on his shoulders. His declaration was encouraging:

You are not the first Frenchman I have met, but I like your words better than those of your fellow-countrymen. What you say of war is true. It brings weeping widows, burned villages, and hungry children. Therefore, I tell you now that we will make no war on the Sioux if they, too, wish to remain at peace. You will be safe to travel westward whenever you choose, but let your fort remain here. We need many things from you and until you came to our country we had to make long journeys by canoe in order to procure them. It is true that peaceful trade is always better than war. It is also true that no man, not even the bravest, ever wishes to risk leaving his scalp in another's tent. Those are my words.

Jean-Baptiste, who had learned enough of the Cree language to follow most of what the chief said, leaned forward and whispered to his father. "His words are fine, but I would have more confidence in them if those scalp locks were not dangling from the seams of his leggings. I've counted them. There are eight."

"This time we'd better hope the chief means what he says," la Verendrye replied. "Within the next few weeks I want to send you northwestward to build what I hope may be one of our last posts. It will be somewhere close to this lake the Indians call Winnipeg. You will be in the heart of the Cree country and, I think, very near the frontiers of the Sioux tribe."

That same spring of 1733, Christophe de la Jemeraye was put in command of four fur-bearing canoes and sent off to Quebec. With him la Verendrye sent a long report and a freshly drawn map. He wrote:

I grow confident we are nearing the Western Sea. Since I have been in this region I have noticed that the prevailing winds are westerly and that they almost invariably bring rain. May not this be the result of condensing moisture that was sucked up from the sea by the heat of the sun?

Later in this same report la Verendrye explained as best he could the temporary delay in his exploration. He knew that Beauharnois would understand, but he felt less confident of Maurepas.

Next spring the Crees have promised to lead me to the villages of a tribe called the Mantannes, or Mandans. They are also known as the Sioux-Who-Live-Underground. These people dwell on the River of the West, so the Crees say, and their country is situated about 1000 miles to the west of Lake of the Woods. They have eight villages surrounded by fields of Indian corn, melons, and pumpkins. Their houses are built of wood and earth like those of the French. I intend to invite these Mantannes to lead me onward until we come to that western end of the sea shown in so many maps and which we have so often discussed, Sire, between ourselves.

The report also contained details of la Verendrye's financial position. Already he had spent a total of $15,000 in cash of his own and credit obtained. Thanks to a better supply of furs this year, he had been able to avoid increasing his debts. Even so, they still amounted to a little under $8,000.

Beauharnois knew that la Verendrye was doing as much as he could. The fact that he had been able to maintain peace among the Indian tribes counted highly. Indian wars, as Beauharnois knew, had an unfortunate habit of spreading like a prairie fire. If such a war chanced to spread eastward, then the French settlements might find themselves in a dangerous situation.

The governor-general wrote his views in a letter to Maurepas. Once again he urged that France provide some financial assistance to this lonely and intrepid explorer who, if nothing else, was doing so much to open up the fur trade for the benefit of the colonies and France herself. Only la Verendrye, added the governor-general, had prevented almost the whole of the Indian fur trade from falling into the hands of the English at Hudson Bay or in the colonies to the south. Only la Verendrye had prevented the outbreak of an Indian war.

The reply Beauharnois received was not encouraging. France was still content to deprive her New World possession of money and freedom. Minister Comte de Maurepas wrote:

I have submitted your correspondence, Monsieur, and that of la Verendrye to His Majesty. His Majesty was kind enough to approve of the establishment of trading posts at Rainy Lake and Lake of the Woods. He welcomes the news that the Cree tribe shows friendliness toward the French. But His Majesty bids me indicate to yourself, Monsieur, that he does not approve of giving financial assistance to la Verendrye as requested in your letter. His Majesty believes that exploration should pay for itself. If the quest for this Western Bay or Gulf proves successful, then, His Majesty declares, he will reward generously those who are responsible.

Twenty-four-year-old King Louis the Fifteenth could not visualize a lonely gray-haired explorer living in a log-walled cabin in the forested wilds of New France. Nor could he and his minister understand why so much money—as much as Louis spent on a modest State banquet!—should be necessary to find an unknown inlet of the sea said to be not too far away. One wonders whether King Louis was even consulted on the matter. France's attitude toward her colony remained that of an old, suspicious, autocratic miser who insisted on interfering and discouraging everything a younger member of the family wished to do.

While Maurepas was composing his reply, la Verendrye was having fresh troubles of his own. In spite of the promise made by Mah-to-he-ha and the other Cree chiefs, these Indians had begun to plan an attack on some of the Sioux tribe. La Verendrye acted swiftly. He had a remarkable facility for getting on well with the Indians, and this quality was of help to him now. He called for the conspiring chiefs, revealed his knowledge of their plans, and sternly forbade them to carry out the proposed attack. Once again the Indians stood in silence as la Verendrye scolded them.

"You are like a small hawk," said one of the chiefs, when la Verendrye finished. "The hawk does not hesitate to attack larger and stronger birds than itself; you do not hesitate to tell us when we are wrong. I tell you now: we will not go on the warpath against the Sioux."

The meeting ended. Two hundred Crees climbed into their canoes to go up Rainy River to their settlement on the shores of Rainy Lake. Somewhere along the river they sighted three Sioux scouts. The Crees immediately assumed— rightly as it happened—that these scouts were with a war party. They opened fire with their muskets. One of the scouts fell dead; the remaining two escaped by disappearing into the forest.

The Crees went back to report to la Verendrye.

"We are lucky that only one Sioux was killed," la Verendrye said. "If you had waited to open fire on the main body of warriors, we would have a war on our hands at once."

While the French remained on the alert for fresh signs of the marauding Sioux, Jean-Baptiste returned from his reconnaissance of the Lake

Winnipeg area. He was quite unimpressed by the fact that he had been in country that was totally unknown to any European. The twenty-year-old Jean-Baptiste was developing into a resourceful explorer. He reported that Lake Winnipeg was rich fur country, but that the Indians were taking their furs overland to the English trading post on James Bay at the southern end of Hudson Bay.

"It's a seven-hundred-mile journey each way for them," Jean-Baptiste reported, "and the trip takes several months. They've heard of our trading post at Lake of the Woods, and they say that they'll bring a few bales of pelts here next spring. I told them they'd be well advised to do so. They can come by the Winnipeg River all the way, and the distance is less than two hundred miles. I saw some of the trade goods they got from the English. The copper kettles, knives, and axes are excellent, and so is the gunpowder."

That summer and fall of 1733 were a bad time for the Frenchmen at Rainy Lake and Lake of the Woods. Heavy rain in the spring almost ruined the wild rice. Only a small crop could be stored for the winter. The Montreal merchants failed to send a convoy of canoes to an arranged meeting place on Lake Superior, even though la Verendrye had been able to arrange cash payment for the goods he ordered. The men were short of coffee, sugar, tobacco, flour, salt, and cooking oil. Heavy rains flooded the lake and muddied the water, so that the Indians could not see to spear the sturgeon that they preserved as a source of food. The Crees and the Assiniboins, like the French *voyageurs*, were irritable and discontented. La Verendrye knew that the Indians were liable to start fighting at any time.

On New Year's Day, 1734, he called them to a general council meeting. Three to four hundred Indians entered the gates in the palisade and arranged themselves in a squatting semicircle in front of la Verendrye, who stood alone to receive them. In the background the other Frenchmen were grouped against the frost-whitened walls of their cabins.

The Cree warriors had ornamented themselves with scarlet war paint for the occasion. Their long black hair was plaited and encased in wrap-

pings of otter skin. Over their bare shoulders they had draped short leather jackets, richly decorated with beads and feathers. Their headdresses were made of feathers, porcupine quills, and strips of fur.

La Verendrye, in his plain deerskin jacket and leather knee pants, made a lonely and unassuming figure. Beside him was planted the flag of France, white with golden lilies. He spoke to the gathering:

Our king is looking far to the west of your country. All that we, his servants, ask of you is that you remain at peace with your neighbors. Only in times of peace can we obey the commands of our king and venture into countries yet unknown to all Frenchmen. If you observe the wishes of our king, he will reward you with presents. But if you go on the warpath, the smoke of burning villages may cause our king to turn his eyes elsewhere. This year I have few presents to give you on behalf of our king. The distance from the French settlements to this Fort Saint Charles at Lake of the Woods is very great and our canoes are few. If you choose to remain at peace, the number of our canoes will increase every year. They will bring you goods of better quality and in greater quantity. Here are the presents from our king for this year.

Jean-Baptiste stepped forward. He removed a bearskin from a pile of trade goods that lay on the frozen ground in front of the Indians. The Crees gazed with delighted eyes on "thirty pounds of gunpowder, forty of ball, two hundred gun-flints, fifteen pounds of tobacco, twenty axes, sixty knives, sixty ramrods, and sixty awls, to-gether with beads, needles, and vermilion paint."

Although la Verendrye and his men were short of food, they had managed during the past three weeks to shoot enough game for the feast that followed.

After giving fresh assurances that they would not go to war, the guests departed to their homes. La Verendrye again had managed to keep peace throughout the countryside, but he was com-pelled to do so at his own expense.

The winter snow melted, and the first shim-mer of green appeared on the trees. As the sun grew warmer, four unknown Crees arrived at Fort Saint Charles.

"We have been sent by our chief who lives on the shores of Lake Winnipeg," they said. "Our chief asks that you hasten to build a trading post there. The young man, your son, who came to visit us last year was the first white man we have seen. Our chief has learned of the trading posts you have established already. Our people are in great need of knives, needles, gunpowder, and lead. What shall we tell our chief?"

La Verendrye saw that the messengers were fed and given a place to sleep. He needed time to think over the reply he should make. He had informed Beauharnois, who in turn informed Maurepas, that this coming year he would try to reach the Mandan country. But fresh complications seemed to arise every time he planned to make a start. There were not enough trade goods left to stock the new post. Fort Saint Pierre at Rainy Lake, as well as Fort Saint Charles, was also short of supplies. There was no guarantee that the Montreal merchants would send everything they had promised to dispatch the previous year. If they failed again, fur trading would come to a standstill and all further exploration would have to be postponed indefinitely. For the first time in his experience, his men would be short of absolute necessities, including even ammunition.

"Tell your chief," la Verendrye said to the Indians next morning, "that I must visit our governor. From him I shall obtain the fresh supplies I need to buy your furs at the new trading post for which you ask. When I return from the Great River, I will come to visit your chief in his own country."

The messengers departed. La Verendrye began his journey to Quebec. He arrived at the settlement on August 16 after spending only a few days with his wife and family at Isle Dupas. His meeting with Beauharnois was the first in three years.

"It is easier to convince me than it is the merchants that exploration is valuable," said the governor-general. "I have been studying the figures for the fur trade. It is clear that you have deflected much of the business from Hudson Bay to Montreal, but our merchants will never appreciate the fact. They are concerned only with the debts you owe them. It is true that you have been able to reduce those debts slightly, but that only makes them the more impatient for final settlement. You know, Monsieur de la Verendrye, I am not sure who worries about you the most: Maurepas, the English fur traders, myself, or the Montreal merchants."

"The merchants here are making a fair profit on the bales of fur I bring every year," said la Verendrye. "As I came down the river this time, I left another twenty bales with them. Once again I have more than covered my expenses and made payment for the fresh supplies I need. But I cannot pay off the debts I contracted in earlier years."

"The merchants may be satisfied," replied Beauharnois, "but I am less confident of Maurepas. It will be hard to explain to the minister why you are not on the way to the Mandans."

"There are times when I find it hard to explain matters to myself," la Verendrye replied. "Seven years have passed since I set out on the first expedition we planned, but we know little more about the supposed route to the Western Sea than we did then. I blame myself for the delays, but when I look back over those years I do not see how else I could have acted at the time."

"I agree with you," said the govenor-general, "but at the same time I must urge you, my friend, to make all haste you can. To keep the Crees content, I think you will have to build the trading post they ask for in the vicinity of Lake Winnipeg. Perhaps one more post after that, well to the south of Winnipeg, and then you will have advanced far enough to the west. From the last of them you will have to strike out in search of that unknown river that may flow to the west. Remember: you are not a young man. You have not many years left as an active explorer."

The Montreal merchants proved obstinate to deal with. They preferred full cashboxes and quick profits to patriotism and the hope of future geographical discoveries. At first they were reluctant to extend the credit that la Verendrye had obtained from them. Finally they agreed and also allowed him to increase his debt by a few hundred dollars.

"By the time you reach your Western Sea," grumbled one of the merchants, "you will have to spend your royal reward to pay off your debts in Montreal. What will you do then, Monsieur de la Verendrye?"

"Perhaps set about the preparation of a great overland route to the west," said la Verendrye. "Forts and staging posts will have to be built at regular intervals along it so that your goods, and those of other merchants, will be able to pass safely from coast to coast."

The trader, Louis d'Ailleboust, looked at him sharply.

"That remark of yours gives me an idea, *monsieur*. The thing we lack at present is any active share in your fur business. Now if, for example, I were managing one of your trading posts and had my own agent stationed there, you would be spared the trouble of running it and have more time for your exploration. We could arrange matters so that I would pay you a share of the profits from the post. In that way you could reduce your debts steadily."

The suggestion was interesting. What la Verendrye really needed was a source of income and freedom from the responsibility of supervis-

ing Fort Saint Pierre at Rainy Lake and perhaps
Fort Saint Charles at Lake of the Woods. As he
moved farther westward, such supervision would
become more and more difficult for him to maintain. Let others take on the work and pay him a
share of the profits. His mind was on those new
posts he hoped to build soon.

There were further discussions among la
Verendrye, d'Ailleboust, and other traders at
Montreal. Agreement was finally reached that
Fort Saint Pierre would be taken over at once.
Fort Saint Charles would change management at
a later date when la Verendrye moved west. For
the time being, however, that particular trading
post would remain under his care. Beauharnois
was informed and gave his permission for this
new arrangement.

The news of the unknown Mandan tribe that
la Verendrye brought to the settlements was
eagerly noted by the Jesuit mission. They asked
if he would agree to allow one of their mission-
aries to accompany him when he set out to locate
that tribe. When la Verendrye began his return

journey to Lake of the Woods in June, 1735, Father Jean-Pierre Aulneau went with him.

The expedition was quite an undertaking for the young missionary. He was born in France and had arrived in the New World only a year earlier. Aulneau was a well-educated man, who already was taking an intelligent interest in the quest for the Western Sea. In a letter, he wrote:

If what is said about the region where the Mandans dwell is true, I believe they are not far from California, for if one is to believe the Indians they are on the banks of a large river that rises and falls with the tide, which goes to show that the sea is not far off. What is this river? That is something not easy to guess. I think, however, that it must be that great river shown by Father Kino, a German Jesuit, on the map he traced of the regions of America lying north of California. He calls it Rio Colorado del Norte.

Another young passenger accompanied la Verendrye on his voyage back to Lake of the Woods.

Eighteen-year-old Louis-Joseph, his youngest

son, was traveling in one of the canoes. The boy had remained at school longer than his three older brothers and received a better education. He was awaiting anxiously a chance to join his father and brothers in the Northwest and now that chance had come. Louis-Joseph was a slimly built, enterprising young fellow with a great deal of common sense and a tremendous interest in exploration.

La Verendrye and his canoes reached Lake of the Woods in September. Although it was late in the year, he detailed la Jemeraye and six of the most reliable *voyageurs* to Lake Winnipeg at once. There they were to build the long-awaited trading post. Louis-Joseph and his older brother, François, accompanied the party.

Both Fort Saint Charles and Fort Saint Pierre at Rainy Lake had prospered during la Verendrye's absence. Thanks to la Jemeraye's activity and initiative, 600 bales of furs now filled the storehouse at Lake of the Woods. Their sale would see la Verendrye through another year and provide him with a small financial reserve.

In his spare time la Jemeraye had been preparing a brief written report about the Mandans. He collected this information from Assiniboin Indians who came to the fort during the summer. Father Aulneau read this report with great eagerness and afterward remarked that he was beginning to feel more optimistic about his mission to that tribe. La Jemeraye wrote:

The Mandans are said to resemble the French. They build their forts like the French and know how to construct drawbridges. They live in seven villages beside a river that is so wide that it is almost impossible to see a man standing on the other side. This river flows in a southwest direction. Down near its mouth live other Indians who wear clothing like that of the white man and use iron tools. They procure these things from white men who come in ships to the mouth of the river.

Father Aulneau was eager to set off to the Mandans at once, but la Verendrye persuaded him to delay his departure. "The Assiniboins are a friendly tribe, but the information they give may not be reliable. Remain here during the winter. Learn all you can about the Indians. Go, if you wish, next spring."

Meanwhile la Jemeraye and his companions traveled over 150 miles along the Winnipeg River, and then went on foot to the Red River. They chose a site close to the banks, a few miles to the south of the southern end of Lake Winnipeg. There, on a small plateau some five miles to the north of the modern town of Selkirk, they labored throughout most of the winter. The new trading post was named Fort Maurepas.

The intense cold and endless labor were too much for la Jemeraye. He was taken seriously ill. Louis-Joseph and François decided to convey him back to Fort Saint Charles, where he would receive better care and attention. These two young men, with little previous experience and entirely ignorant of the country through which they were passing, transported the sick man as far as the Winnipeg River. Placing him in a canoe, they paddled more than half of the distance to Lake of the Woods when la Jemeraye's condition became worse. Louis-Joseph and François made camp ashore, wrapped him warmly in furs, and laid him on a couch beside the fire. There was nothing else they could do.

Four days later, on May 10, 1736, Christophe de la Jemeraye died. He was buried beside the Winnipeg River. Louis-Joseph and François reached Fort Saint Charles on June 4.

6
Massacre Island

The news of la Jemeraye's death came as a great shock to la Verendrye. His nephew had been an energetic and reliable second-in-command. He was to have remained at Lake of the Woods while la Verendrye set off for the Mandan country. La Jemeraye also would have prepared Fort Saint Pierre for handing over to the agent who soon would be due to arrive from Montreal.

Now all the plans would have to be changed. La Verendrye decided that he must remain at Lake of the Woods while Jean-Baptiste would command the canoes taking the bales of fur to Michilimackinac. At that trading post, he was to buy certain needed stores and then return as quickly as he could. La Verendrye realized that otherwise the expedition to the Mandans might have to be postponed once again. This delay would create the worst kind of impression on Beauharnois and the impatient Maurepas.

Jean-Baptiste took twenty men in four canoes with him. Father Aulneau went along as a passenger, apparently intending to return to Montreal. The young missionary had decided that la Verendrye would be unable to go to the Mandan country in the near future and was against anyone trying to go there on his own. He was beginning to realize that Canada was a much larger and more dangerous place, the Indians more intractable, than he had believed in the civilized surroundings of France. Father Aulneau had come to the conclusion that he could perform more useful labors in the colony beside the Saint Lawrence.

La Verendrye had a strange presentiment about the outcome of this trip to Michilimackinac. He stood on the shore to watch while the canoes were made ready and the men took their places. "Stay on your guard all the time," he called to twenty-three-year-old Jean-Baptiste. "Always camp on an island at night, if you can. Don't allow more than one canoe to approach you closely when you're out on the lake. And never withdraw the charges from your muskets unless you have reason to believe that the powder needs replacing."

Jean-Baptiste looked at him from his canoe. "You seem worried. Why?"

La Verendrye shrugged. "There was an Indian here at the fort early this morning. He told me that there's a rumor among his people that a Sioux war party is heading into this area. It may be just gossip, but it's better to be careful."

The canoes paddled off across the lake. La Verendrye remained restless and ill at ease. He ordered the thirty Frenchmen at the post not to go far away; they were to load their muskets and keep them handy in their sleeping quarters. A man was ordered into each of the high lookout platforms, one of which stood at each corner of the rectangular palisade, and told to give the alarm if any party of Indians was seen approaching.

A Frenchman named René Bourassa had left Fort Saint Charles several days earlier. Bourassa, who was accompanied by his Sioux wife and three other Indians, had been given permission by la Verendrye to go to Rainy Lake. Bourassa told him that he wanted to enquire after some personal belongings that had been sent to him by his family in Montreal. He believed that the packages might have been overlooked at Fort Saint Pierre.

Somewhere along the river Bourassa was ambushed by Sioux as he stepped ashore from his canoe. The Crees with him managed to dive into the river and escaped by swimming underwater. The war party plundered Bourassa's belongings and lashed him to a tree. As they prepared to set about torturing him, his wife called out, "My kinsmen, why are you doing this to my husband? He has always treated me well. If you want to capture Frenchmen, then you have only to take your canoes and go out on the lake to meet them coming this way."

The Sioux released Bourassa and allowed him to continue his journey to Fort Saint Pierre. The war party then set off for Lake of the Woods.

Jean-Baptiste remembered his father's instructions. As evening of the first day approached, he directed the canoes to an island (now called Massacre Island) less than a mile long and a few hundred yards wide. The Frenchmen camped there for the night. Next morning they drank coffee, ate their rations, and began to reload their canoes. They were suddenly interrupted by a war whoop. Jumping to their feet they saw a number of Sioux warriors charging toward them from the far side of the island, which they had managed to reach unseen in the faint light of dawn.

The Frenchmen reached for their muskets and pistols. They opened fire as soon as the Indians were within thirty yards' range. Several of the Sioux fell dead or wounded, but the war party continued its onward rush. There was no time to reload. The French used their muskets as clubs and defended themselves as best they could. One by one they were struck down. Jean-Baptiste was one of the last to fall.

During the first few moments of the attack, Father Aulneau apparently reacted as an ordinary man in danger of his life. He seized a light ax with which to defend himself, then dropped it as he recalled his religious vocation and sank to his knees. An arrow took him in the chest, and a tomahawk ended his life.

Six days after the massacre, Cree Indians arrived at Fort Saint Charles with news of the event. La Verendrye immediately sent out a search party, which included nineteen-year-old Louis-Joseph. The bodies were found lying where they had fallen, that of Father Aulneau with a crucifix in his hands and the discarded ax beside him. There was no trace of the Sioux, even though war parties of Crees patrolled several hundred square miles of country in search of them. The bodies were brought back to Fort Saint Charles and interred within the stockade.

This second tragedy almost destroyed la Verendrye. First la Jemeraye, now Jean-Baptiste.

There was no one left on whom he could rely to look after Fort Saint Charles and Fort Saint Pierre. The newly finished trading post of Maurepas still had to be stocked with trade goods. Pierre, the eldest surviving son, was twenty-two years old. He was becoming a veteran woodsman, but he lacked interest in the fur trade and had no wish to take over one of the posts. François was slow and not very bright, dependable in his quiet way but lacking initiative. Louis-Joseph was the most intelligent of the three boys and certainly the best educated. Yet he was happier when off in the wilds. Left at a trading post for any length of time, he soon became bored.

For two months after the massacre Cree delegations came to Fort Saint Charles almost daily. They urged la Verendrye to join with them in an avenging war party to attack the Sioux. His steadfast refusal surprised and disappointed them. La Verendrye wrote to Beauharnois:

We must keep the peace between our own Indians and the Sioux. Therefore, I have abandoned my first hasty idea to unite with the Crees in a war against those Sioux of the plains. Now I am again working to keep the peace between the two nations, so that the fur trade may continue to prosper and conditions throughout this region become stable again. But until such conditions are achieved, any expedition passing through Sioux country to the Mandans certainly would be exposed to constant overpowering attacks.

Louis-Joseph was sent off with six men to open the trading post at Fort Maurepas. La Verendrye remained at Fort Saint Charles. Daily he continued to pacify and influence the Crees. By the fall of the year 1736 he knew that his influence had prevented hostilities with the Sioux. Once again the nations were in a state of peace. In September, an agent and several men arrived from Montreal to take over the trading post at Rainy Lake. La Verendrye's difficulties gradually were clearing. He decided that the time had come to make his next move.

On February 8, 1737, he set off with Pierre and François for Fort Maurepas. They were accompanied by ten *voyageurs* and eight Indians with their wives. The most reliable *voyageur* was left with twenty other men to hold Fort Saint Charles during his absence.

After a winter journey down the Winnipeg River, they reached Fort Maurepas on February 25. La Verendrye was now in his fifty-second year, which, in those times, was considered an age at which a man should remain close to his fireside. But no sooner had he arrived at the post than he was holding meetings with the Indians, writing a long report to Governor-General Beauharnois, and preparing for the western journey of which he had dreamed.

Once again his plans were ruined. Indians coming back to Fort Maurepas from the Hudson Bay area brought with them an epidemic of smallpox. Large numbers of the local Indians died. The *voyageurs* with la Verendrye refused to accompany him any farther into unknown territory while the epidemic still lingered.

"If we must die," they said bluntly, "let it be in the company of our own comrades, with a roof and not the cold sky above us, and a proper bed on which to lie. We have no wish to die a heathen death beside some unmarked trail in the wilderness. In this fort we would receive proper Christian burial and our graves be given respect."

Murderous war parties, raging smallpox, a chronic shortage of trade goods, and unmapped country meant little to Comte Jean-Frédéric de Maurepas. He reflected that he had yet to receive a report to indicate that la Verendrye had set out on his journey to the Western Sea. Maurepas assumed, therefore, that la Verendrye was not making any serious effort to get there. He wrote to Beauharnois:

> It grieved me to learn of the unhappy deaths of Monsieur la Verendrye's son and of those twenty Frenchmen who died with him. However that may be, all that has come to my knowledge as to the causes of the misadventure confirms the suspicions I have always entertained, and which I have not concealed from you, that the beaver trade has more to do than anything else with Monsieur de la Verendrye's Western Sea expedition.

Beauharnois puzzled how to answer this letter. He had to keep the minister happy, and at the same time he wished to continue doing what he could for la Verendrye. Seemingly from now on any official assistance he gave to the explorer would have to be kept secret from the suspicious Maurepas. As the first step, he sent for a bold and adventurous young man named Charles Lamarque, who had a certain amount of land and wealth of his own.

"La Verendrye needs another experienced leader," Beauharnois told him. "He is laboring under a constant handicap since he lost la Jemeraye and Jean-Baptiste. I believe strongly that if you suddenly arrived in his territory with some good men, he would welcome your assistance. La Verendrye is not a greedy man, and probably he would allow you some share of the pelts he collects yearly. He already has reached a similar arrangement in connection with Fort Saint Pierre, but I think someone reliable should be at Lake of the Woods too."

Lamarque organized a small fleet of canoes, engaged the best *voyageurs* he could find, and procured a heavy stock of trade goods. After covering a distance of about 2000 miles, he reached

Fort Saint Charles in the early summer of 1738. La Verendrye had returned to that fort only a week previously, accompanied by the *voyageurs* who were so scared of smallpox.

Beauharnois had made an accurate prediction. Lamarque, a big, slow-moving young man of twenty-seven, and tough, gray-haired little la Verendrye made friends at once. They came to a private arrangement whereby Fort Saint Charles and Fort Maurepas would be stocked with the trade goods Lamarque brought, and Lamarque would receive a share of the profits on the fur business. La Verendrye had greatly reduced his active interest in the trading posts and was able again to think and plan freely.

As the smallpox was waning steadily and no new cases had been reported for the past month, the western expedition now became a matter for urgent consideration. Fort Saint Charles was to be left in the charge of the men who had done well during la Verendrye's recent absence at Fort Maurepas. Lamarque and la Verendrye would lead a party west. During their journey they would erect two new trading posts to the west of the Red River, the Rio Colorado del Norte. These stations would cater to Indians who, for one reason or another, would not take their furs to Fort Maurepas in Cree country.

7
Westward

Final preparations for the western expedition were made when the party completed the first stage of their journey to Fort Maurepas. Extra men who had been brought from Fort Saint Charles were set to work building two new forts to be named Fort Rouge and Fort La Reine. The first was located at the junction of the Assiniboine River and the Red River; the second was another 100 miles farther to the west on the Assiniboine River.

La Verendrye and fifty-one well-armed com-

panions set out October 20, 1738. Young Pierre
de la Verendrye remained in charge of Fort
Maurepas, but François and Louis-Joseph accompanied their father. A number of Assiniboins volunteered to go with the expedition, and twenty-
five of them were chosen. Lamarque was second-
in-command.

The party was venturing into utterly unknown country, so they had to rely on the ser-
vices of Indian guides. Heading westward, they
began a long and monotonous march across the
prairie. Autumn was well under way. The land
had been so dried by months of summer sun that
clouds of dust rose beneath the men's feet and
clung to their faces and clothing. The *voyageurs*
were more accustomed to water than they were
to dry, flat, and uninteresting country. They
soon became morose and irritable under the
weight of their packs and muskets. Their only
consolation was that they were following the
course of the wide and meandering Assiniboine
River. Although the river contained frequent
sandbanks and was almost impossible to navigate,
it provided compensations. Along the banks grew

splendid trees where the Frenchmen found pleasant spots in which to camp for the night. In the river itself were pools where they could remove the dust.

At the spot where the modern town of Portage la Prairie stands, the guides told la Verendrye that they must turn southwest, which meant leaving the river behind them. Afterward conditions became worse. From then on there were only occasional rivulets or springs, and there was no shade at all to protect the explorers during the noonday halt.

Conditions improved when they reached the Pembina Mountains in the northeast corner of North Dakota. The wind blew more coolly, water was more abundant, and the nights were cold. Another 200 miles farther on, the dusty, long-haired men in their heavy clothing were able to wash away the grime and much of their discontent in the chilling waters of the Souris River.

La Verendrye was growing impatient with the slow progress of the march. Mid-November had arrived, and the principal Indian guide on whom they were relying seemed to become more vague every day. Time, distance, plans, and schedules meant nothing to him.

"Have I not done well?" he asked proudly at the end of a two-day detour to the south. "See, I have brought you to a spot where there is plenty of buffalo. The river that flows to the west? Oh, we will march toward it tomorrow after we have eaten well tonight."

"But when will we reach the Mandan villages that are said to be beside that river?" asked la Verendrye.

The Indian shrugged. "Maybe another four marches. Maybe another eight. What does it matter as long as we eat well during our journey?"

"It matters quite a lot," replied la Verendrye. "I want to reach the Mandans in time to prepare for the onset of winter, since we will not have time to return to our posts beside the Red River."

Seven days and a hundred miles later, they sighted the first of the Mandan villages. It came as a great shock to la Verendrye. In spite of his habitual skepticism, he had heard so much about

the Mandans over the year that unconsciously he
had come to expect a people more like Europeans.

Toward sunset on that particular day they saw
ahead of them a neat cluster of earth and wicker-
work huts lining both sides of what appeared to
be a wide and well-kept street. Out from this
village came a party of Indians whose only gar-
ment consisted of a buffalo robe draped casually
round their shoulders. Standing in the well-shaped
doorways of the cottages were women, dressed
more elaborately than the men in soft buckskin
jackets and knee-length dresses of the same ma-
terial.

"Behold," the chief guide said to la Verendrye.
"The Mandans are coming to greet us."

La Verendrye reported to Beauharnois:

> I confess I was greatly surprised as I expected to
> see people quite different from the other savages
> according to the stories that had been told us. They
> do not differ from the Assiniboin, being naked ex-
> cept for a garment of buffalo skin carelessly worn
> without any breechcloth. I knew then that I could
> rely on little of all that had been told me.

Whatever his disappointment, la Verendrye saw that his party made an impressive entrance into this strange village.

> I made one of my sons take the flag showing in colors the arms of France and march at the head, while our Frenchmen were directed to follow in proper marching order.

This little parade so delighted the cheerful and good-natured Mandans that they insisted on removing la Verendrye from his place in the column and carried him on their shoulders into the main street. They set him down at the entrance to their chief's large and very well-built house.

Whoever these Mandans were, the people were much advanced in their ways compared with the Crees and Assiniboins with whom la Verendrye was familiar. Their language was completely different and incomprehensible to him. Fortunately, two of the Assiniboins with the French also spoke a smattering of the Mandan tongue, and Louis-Joseph, who had a gift for learning languages, spoke the Assiniboin dialect fluently. The young man took a particular liking

to the Mandans, and although he shared his
father's disappointment he was delighted with
the thought that they had encountered a new and
hitherto entirely unknown tribe of Indians.

"They're more intelligent than the Crees and
Assiniboins," he said, "which probably explains
why their houses are so much better. Also, their
skins are a different color, their customs and hab-
its are very advanced, and they have a great preference for cleanliness and order. I think those are
the reasons why the Indians in the country
around the Great Lakes described them as a white
race. They're certainly not an ordinary Indian
tribe."

La Verendrye was inclined to agree with
Louis-Joseph. He believed that at some time in
their history the Mandans must have been exposed to European ways.

We found that there were about 130 cabins in
the village. All the streets, squares, and cabins are
similar in appearance; often our Frenchmen would
lose their way in going about. They keep the streets
and open spaces very clean; the ramparts are smooth
and wide; the palisade is supported on crosspieces

mortised into posts fifteen feet apart. Their central
fort is built on slightly higher ground and surrounded with a ditch over fifteen feet deep and
from fifteen to eighteen feet wide. Entrance to this
fort is only obtained by steps or pieces of wood,
which they remove when threatened by the enemy.
Their fortification, indeed, has nothing savage
about it.

The whole tribe is very industrious. Their dwell-
ings are large and spacious, divided into several
apartments with wide planks. Nothing is lying
about; all their belongings are placed in large bags
hung on posts. Their beds are made in the form of
tombs and are surrounded by skins. Their fort is
very well provided with cellars, where they store
all they have in the way of grains, meat, fat, dressed
skins, and bearskins. They have a great stock of
these things, which form the money of the country.

Through his Assiniboin interpreters la Verendrye collected more information. He was told
that on the banks of the almost legendary River
of the West, as the Missouri River was known,
there were several Mandan settlements, all of
them larger than this present one. The nearest of
those settlements was not more than a day's jour-

ney away. Beyond the Mandans lived a tribe named the Panaux.

Beyond the Panaux again, said the interpreter, another tribe lived beside a river so wide that one could not see across it. Its water was too salty to be drinkable. This unknown tribe included skilled metalworkers. Their skins were white, and they wore a kind of armor that was proof against arrows. They protected themselves with spears and swords, and they lived in houses built of stone. The interpreters were impressed with the fact that this tribe was skilled in the use of the horse, an animal yet to be introduced among the Mandans.

Once again la Verendrye could not make sense of this strange rigmarole. Seemingly the Mandans *must* be describing the Spanish on the shores of the Gulf of Mexico. Had he come too far south with his guides? Should they have followed some more northerly river that did indeed flow to the west?

Louis-Joseph had a very definite opinion on the matter. "When the Indians speak of the River of the West," he said, "I believe that they mean the river that flows *from* the west and not *to* the west. It seems to me that if we followed the river upstream we'd be moving in a more westerly direction than we have been up to the present."

His sense of geography was very keen. If his father had chosen to ascend the Missouri River, which was now within a few miles of them, they would have neared the western boundary of Montana and thus reached the formidable barrier of the Rocky Mountains. The sight of those great ranges would have convinced la Verendrye that the French dream of an inlet leading to the Western Sea was impossible.

But la Verendrye was confused. The Mandans were insistent that he should head toward the southwest. He himself believed, like Louis-Joseph, that they should take a westerly direction. While he was almost certain that the Missouri River joined the Mississippi River and flowed into the well-known Gulf of Mexico, the Mandans stated that the nearby river flowed to the southwest.

At last he reached a decision. "Take some men

with you," he said to Louis-Joseph. "Go with
Mandan guides until you reach their village by
the river. Take a compass bearing and discover
which way the river actually flows. I will remain
here with the rest of the party until you return."

Louis-Joseph set off with seven Frenchmen
and two Mandan warriors. On the second day
out they reached the Missouri near the modern
town of Mandan. The entire population of the
village turned out to give a good-natured welcome to the first white men they ever had seen.
They watched with great interest while Louis-
Joseph took a careful compass bearing on the
course of the river. He discovered that it flowed
southwest by south. By sheer bad luck there were
high bluffs farther downstream, and they prevented him from seeing that the river soon returned to its normal southeasterly course.

Louis-Joseph and his companions returned
with the news to the village where la Verendrye
was awaiting them. Both father and son still continued to have doubts.

"Next spring we must go farther westward
and try to discover some more promising river,"

said la Verendrye. "I think that by following this present one, we are certain to reach territory already known to Europeans. The Mandans are eager for us to remain here during the winter. We'll start off again as soon as travel becomes possible next spring."

La Verendrye's plans for the spring of 1739 were abruptly ruined. His two Assiniboin interpreters unexpectedly announced their wish to return home. One of them declared that his wife was unhappy among this strange tribe; the other said that he wished to return in order to marry an Assiniboin girl. Without these two men, the Frenchmen would be unable to understand anything the Mandans said to them.

December had arrived and the increasing intensity of the snowfalls indicated that an exceptionally cold winter was on the way. La Verendrye knew that he would have to travel quickly in order to complete the return journey before blizzards became a deadly threat.

The difficulty about interpreters must not occur again. La Verendrye made up his mind about that matter. He chose two Frenchmen, one of whom was able to read and write, and arranged for them to stay in the Mandan village until he returned the following summer. These Frenchmen were quite willing to undertake their mission. The Mandan women were excellent cooks, and life in their village was more comfortable than the harsh existence at the trading posts.

La Verendrye and his companions set out on December 13. They had waited until almost too late. Intense cold cut down their daily rate of progress, fuel was usually difficult to find, and game scarce. While they were still 200 miles from the newly completed outpost of Fort La Reine on the Assiniboine River, la Verendrye developed pneumonia. As his condition grew worse, Lamarque decided to hasten on to the post in order to obtain a sledge, some extra men, and a supply of foodstuffs. He was returning with these things when he met la Verendrye and the men who had remained with him. The tough old explorer's condition had improved. Too stubborn to admit his weakness, he insisted on walking the remaining distance to the fort.

"When the times comes that I no longer can

finish what I have begun," he said, "I shall retire to a comfortable rocking chair at home. Another year or two, perhaps, but there are still things left for me to do."

The whole party reached Fort La Reine on February 10, 1739. Several of the men were afflicted with snow blindness, and nearly all of them were suffering from frostbite. No sooner were they within the stockade than la Verendrye collapsed again. Throughout that year he was obliged to remain at the trading post while he fought to regain his old-time health and vigor.

8
The Young Explorer

During each of the past three or four years la
Verendrye's financial position had shown a slight
improvement. He was now responsible only for
the three new forts on the western side of the
Red River: Fort Maurepas, Fort Rouge, and
Fort La Reine. The Montreal traders who had
taken over practically all control of his earlier
posts were operating them efficiently and paying
him a share of the modest profits. But there were
certain other traders in Montreal to whom la
Verendrye still owed money from his earlier

years of misfortune. Having heard that his finances were in a more healthy state, they became impatient for immediate settlement of their outstanding accounts.

The row that blew up in Montreal was a classic. A certain François de Lorme claimed $4000. Other smaller but equally impatient creditors claimed a total of $3000. These sums were huge in the days when a good musket could be bought for $8 and a stone-built six-roomed house cost $400. The clamor reached the ears of Beauharnois. In the interests of justice he had to issue an order that the next consignment of furs received from la Verendrye was to be seized and sold on behalf of his creditors.

The order was carried out. When some of la Verendrye's canoes arrived at Michilmackinac in the spring of 1740, a cargo of furs worth $3000 was taken by a bailiff appointed for that purpose. The canoe men were forced to return home without the stores and trade goods that were needed for the new outposts to remain in business.

"I must go to Quebec at once," said la Verendrye, when he heard this disastrous news. "But there is no reason why further exploration should be delayed while I am absent."

Pierre was detailed to take two Frenchmen and return to the Mandan village. Louis-Joseph was placed in command of Fort Rouge. Lamarque would serve as la Verendrye's representative in the whole territory while the leader was absent.

La Verendrye reached Montreal on August 25, 1740. He arrived too late to see his wife. Quiet, patient Marie-Anne had died a few months earlier and now lay buried in Montreal's church of Notre Dame. She had little to bequeath to her family at the time of her death. Most of her money and land titles had been disposed of in past years in order to help her husband's never-ending quest.

Governor Beauharnois received la Verendrye in the kindest way. "It is too late for you to think of returning to the Northwest this year," he said. "You and I grow no younger with the passage of years. Already you have nearly died in a blizzard. This winter you must remain as a guest at my house."

La Verendrye was in a bitter mood. The Montreal traders had helped him in past years while Maurepas was his sour and impatient critic. Now the traders had turned against him, but Maurepas was showing a new interest in exploration.

"If only the ministers and the traders could reach common cause with me at the same time," said la Verendrye, "then there would be a great chance to open up the West."

Recently Maurepas had written:

> I feel that now Monsieur de la Verendrye is pushing farther into hitherto unexplored country, he may stand a good chance of reaching the Western Sea. His idea of leaving two Frenchmen with the Mandan people was a very sound one. With the aid of these new interpreters, he should be able to carry on his search during the coming year. Geographers and others with whom I have consulted continue to be of the opinion that Monsieur de la Verendrye's quest is a worthy one. I take pride in the fact that the flag of our country is being shown in new regions where hitherto it was never displayed.

Still Maurepas made no mention of any official financial assistance for la Verendrye. Between costly warfare with England and the costly pleasures of Versailles, King Louis had no money to spend on exploration in a colony 3000 miles away from France.

La Verendrye's bitter mood influenced the letter he wrote to Maurepas:

> People do not know me; money has never been my object. I have sacrificed myself and my sons for the service of His Majesty and the good of the colony. What advantages shall result from my labors, the future may tell. In all my misfortunes I have the consolation of seeing that the governor-general enters into my views, recognizes the uprightness of my intentions, and continues to do me justice in spite of the opposition of certain parties.

By a series of involved transactions, la Verendrye managed to secure another moderate loan from backers who were impressed by the quantity and quality of the bales of fur arriving from his westerly trading posts. But the need to acquire fresh debts was unfortunate.

On June 26, 1741, la Verendrye, now a white-haired veteran of fifty-six, left Montreal for the last time. He was still as tough as many men ten

years younger than himself. Long periods of intense cold, his active life at the trading posts, and
the simple existence he had led in the wilds had
given him a hardy constitution. But pneumonia
had weakened him. As he went back to the
Northwest he realized that his physical strength
was diminishing. There could be no more long
journeys on foot for him.

The Crees and Assiniboins had made the most
of la Verendrye's absence. During his trip to
Montreal they formed a war party and invaded
Sioux territory, where they fought a heavy battle
with that tribe. Seventy Sioux were killed. The
attackers declared boastfully—and probably un-
truthfully—that they had lost only six men. They
did, however, return to their own country with
more than one hundred captives.

Another piece of discouraging news was that
Pierre and his companions had returned from the
Mandan village without having accomplished any
worthwhile discovery. Still, they had made a
tremendous southward march that took them almost to the Gulf of Mexico until skirmishes with
hostile Indian tribes forced them to retreat. The

two Frenchmen who had been left at the Mandan village returned with Pierre. They declared that they were now fairly proficient in the language of that excellent tribe.

"I do not know why you marched to the south," la Verendrye rebuked his son. "You knew that we decided while we were at the Mandan village that nothing could be gained by going in that direction. France is interested in the discovery of a practicable route leading to the Western Sea. Her ships are already quite capable of finding their way to the Gulf of Mexico. It is to the west, and only to the west, that we must try to go on future journeys."

Pierre was sent off to resume management of a trading post. La Verendrye sent for Louis-Joseph, and with this bright and enterprising twenty-five-year-old son he began to plan a new expedition.

"Go beyond the Mandan villages," la Verendrye said. "Make a final sweep of the territory that lies to the west of them and try to locate some new and more promising river. If you are forced to return, do so by a more southerly route until you reach the Missouri River. Find out the compass course it really follows."

The journey was not the one that Louis-Joseph would have planned for himself. His eyes and thoughts were drifting constantly to the northern end of Lake Winnipeg and the unknown rivers that might proceed westward from there. His intuition as an explorer told him that a more promising route lay in that direction. He remained silent, however, and began to make his preparations.

He chose Édouard la Londette and Jean-Baptiste Amiotte as his companions. Both were hardy veterans who had spent several years at the trading posts. During the first journey to the Mandans la Londette and Amiotte had shown discipline, courage, and endurance.

François, Louis-Joseph's twenty-seven-year-old brother, was also selected. He never would make a leader, but he was a stolid, sensible follower and always prepared to do as he was told.

Louis-Joseph left Fort La Reine on April 29, 1742. Once again they endured the arroyo-slashed desert land rimmed by the heated buttes of North Dakota. They reached the first Mandan village beside the Little Knife River in the middle of May. Three weeks later they were at the second Mandan village beside the muddy yellow waters of the Missouri River. After spending another two weeks there, waiting for guides whom the Mandan villagers said would arrive soon, Louis-Joseph became impatient. Taking with him a couple of Mandans instead, Louis-Joseph crossed the Missouri River and prepared to head west.

The Mandan guides insisted on going toward the southwest. Louis-Joseph, who now spoke the language reasonably well, grew suspicious.

"If we go west, we certainly all will be killed," the Mandans declared. "It is much safer for us to travel southwest."

With this simple statement, they relapsed into silence. Louis-Joseph was unable to obtain any more information from them, but his suspicions remained. "It was my belief," he noted in his log, "that the Mandans, being very good eaters,

preferred to follow a southwesterly course because the country is more fertile in that direction
and game a lot more plentiful."

Young Louis-Joseph was too harsh in his judg-
ment of the Mandan's reasons. Those western
plains were too dangerous to be crossed by a
handful of strangers, European or Indian. A hundred years after Louis-Joseph's journey, European pioneers were still experiencing the hostility
of the westerly tribes.

For twenty days the Frenchmen continued
their monotonous and exhausting march across
the arid prairies. The midday sun blazed down
with unrelenting heat. There was no shade anywhere except among the trees that grew along
the banks of the rivers. Across the desolate expanse of North Dakota they maintained their
southwesterly course. They passed fifty miles to
the east of the future site of Miles City in Montana, crossed the Powder River, and trudged into
the yet unborn state of Wyoming. Indians were
few, but great herds of buffalo wandered across
the plain. As the men cooked their buffalo meat
around a campfire in the evenings, wolves howled

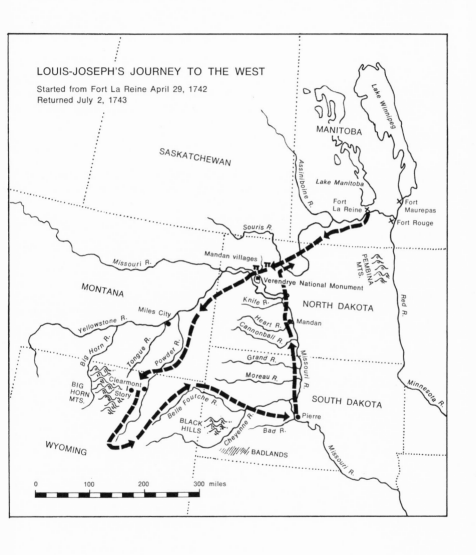

LOUIS-JOSEPH'S JOURNEY TO THE WEST

Started from Fort La Reine April 29, 1742
Returned July 2, 1743

in the distance. Their calls were the only sound to break the silence of the dark midnight hours when a sentinel stood guard over his sleeping companions.

On August 2 they reached a hill that was known locally as the Mountain of the Horse Indians. It was probably somewhere between the Wyoming towns of Story and Clearmont. At this stage the two Mandans became frightened and refused to go farther into the mountainous country that lay ahead.

"Then we'll build a camp here and wait until some other Indians arrive," said Louis-Joseph, after vainly arguing with them. "They may be able to give us information about the country and the tribes to the west."

They built a cabin and lived in it for a month. One Mandan set off by himself to return to his village, but the second and braver one agreed to remain with the Frenchmen until another Indian group appeared.

On September 2 a party of fine-looking Crow Indians arrived. The remaining Mandan promptly took himself off, and Louis-Joseph was left to

deal with the leader of these strangers. He could
not understand the Crow language, but he managed to let the chief know that he wanted guides
to lead him to the Horse Indians, who, he believed, lived even farther to the west.

"I know little of that tribe," replied the chief.
"But I will find guides to take you to a settle-
men of the Little Foxes (Cheyennes), who are
friendly and may know more about those Horse
Indians."

On October 9 Louis-Joseph and his three companions set out with these guides. The course was
still southwesterly, and this fact aroused fresh
doubt in Louis-Joseph's mind.

"With every step we take, we're drawing
nearer to the Pacific Ocean, which is already
known to all Europeans," he said. "I suspect even
more strongly than before that this gulf or inlet
of which we have heard so much lies nowhere so
far south. If it exists at all, then I am sure that it
is at the end of a route leading westward from
Lake Superior."

They reached the Little Foxes on October 11.
At their village they obtained fresh guides and

reached a settlement of the Horse Indians on October 19. Louis-Joseph arrived at a bad time. These Horse Indians had just been attacked by the Snake tribe (Comanches) and suffered great losses.

"Only last year," said the chief, "the Snakes destroyed seventeen of our villages. After they killed most of the warriors, they took many young women as prisoners and sold them as slaves to tribes who live near the seacoast in exchange for tools and horses and weapons made of iron."

Louis-Joseph's gift for learning Indian languages was becoming useful. He had mastered enough of the dialects of this new region to make himself understood reasonably well. Now he was able to ask a question that had puzzled him for a long time.

"Why is it," he said, "that since we left our country far to the northeast, we have not found any guides who will lead us to the west? Always they insist on marching in a southwesterly direction."

The chief gestured toward the setting sun. "In that direction is the country of the Snakes," he replied. "They are why no Indian of the eastern tribes will go west. Although they may be ashamed to say so, the men of all tribes know something of that great and deadly enemy. But to the southwest of us lives a good tribe called the Bows, who do not fear the Snakes. They have horses and mules and donkeys and are very great warriors indeed. I think they may be able to tell you something about this saltwater bay for which you are searching but of which I have not heard a word."

On November 21 the tireless Louis-Joseph led his weary companions into a village of the Bows. The French had a natural gift, often lacking among the English, of being able to make friends quickly with almost any Indian tribe they met. This time they found the Bows friendly and hospitable.

"We are preparing to march westward in the direction of the great ranges (Rocky Mountains)," the chief told Louis-Joseph. "Do not hesitate to come with us. We hope to go so far and climb so high that you will be able to see the ocean for which you have been searching. White people live on that coast far to the south. They have good houses, breed many fine animals including horses, and are very expert at tilling the land. I know a few words of their language."

The chief then spoke some foreign words. Louis-Joseph recognized them as Spanish. Now he knew for sure that he had come too far south. The inlet, if it existed, must indeed lie many hundreds of miles to the north on that western coast, otherwise the Spanish would have discovered it already for themselves.

Louis-Joseph was not eager to take part in the vast war party, which consisted of over 2000 warriors. But he was anxious to be able to say later that he had seen the ocean of which the chief had spoken. Indeed, none of the four ever had seen any ocean, and the fact that they might now do so would be a matter of pride when they returned to the trading posts of the Red and Assiniboine Rivers. Even in Montreal and the other settlements, many of the colonists never had traveled as far as the mouth of the Saint Lawrence River and viewed the Atlantic Ocean.

"My friends and I came to your tents with

peace in our hearts," Louis-Joseph said to the chief. "But because you have become our friends, and because these Snakes are such pitiless enemies of the eastern tribes, we will agree to go with you."

The chief surveyed the four Frenchmen. "With your long hair, your deerskin jackets, and your white faces so darkened by the sun," he said, "the Snake warriors will not be able to distinguish you from our own warriors. The only difference about you is the muskets you carry and the pistols in your belts."

The westward march took place during December. On January 8, 1743, the Bows halted early in the afternoon and began to prepare a base camp for the women and children and surplus baggage. From now on the warriors would go forward alone.

The next morning dawned cold, bright, and crystal clear. In the serene and cloudless light, the Frenchmen suddenly observed distant, snow-white peaks gleaming against the rain-washed blue of the western sky. Behind the massive bulk of Wyoming's Big Horn Mountains, still other

peaks soared upward to solid, majestic heights. Squatting by their campfire, the Frenchmen gazed in silent wonder at these unknown mountains. Many thoughts passed through their minds: the enormous but unexpected width of this whole continent, the impossibility of finding a navigable river through that giant barrier, the insignificance of their own puny efforts to explore the region.

"It's not rivermen you'll need to reach the Western Sea," la Londette said tersely. "Only mountaineers can find a way through yonder ranges."

Those four Frenchmen were the first Europeans to see the Rocky Mountains, the existence of which was entirely unsuspected by European geographers. Their discovery brought to a sudden end France's dream of a new route to the Western Sea. With this one journey, young Louis-Joseph rendered obsolete all earlier maps of North America.

Later that same morning the Bow warriors prepared to begin their stealthy and warlike advance. Louis-Joseph detailed François to stay in the base camp in order to watch over their own

meager supplies. He and the two *voyageurs* went
on with the war party.

On January 12 the Bow scouts reported that a
Snake encampment lay close to the foothills of
some mountains in the near distance. They added
that after making a careful reconnaissance they
discovered that the place was entirely deserted.

This development was something the Bows
had not anticipated. They could not understand
why the Snakes were absent. Slowly and fear-
fully they began to suspect that the enemy might
have learned of their approach and circled around
them in order to attack the baggage camp.

This alarming thought destroyed the warriors'
eagerness for battle. Every man among them began to fear for the safety of his family. The Bows
went into a panic, turned about, and began a
hasty, disorganized retreat. Louis-Joseph, la Londette, and Amiotte were unable to keep up
with the fast-running warriors. Gradually they
dropped behind the rest of the party.

Louis-Joseph suddenly noticed that the other
two men were no longer with him. He went back
alone and found them resting by a creek and

cooking a meal. Before approaching his companions, Louis-Joseph carefully scanned the surrounding country. Suddenly he saw a party of
about fifteen Snake warriors creeping toward the
Frenchmen along a line of bushes.

Louis-Joseph cocked his musket and shouted
an alarm. La Londette and Amiotte dropped their
food, grabbed their own muskets, and rolled into
cover. As they did so, the Snakes leaped to their
feet and began to charge.

All three Frenchmen had double-shotted their
muskets. They allowed the warriors to come
within twenty yards' range, and then fired almost simultaneously. Their shots brought down
several of the Snakes, but the survivors still came
on. The three Frenchmen drew pistols from their
belts and fired again. Amiotte and la Londette
then jumped to their feet and clubbed two more
warriors, while Louis-Joseph dispatched another.
The six remaining Indians fled.

Louis-Joseph noted in his diary:

> The musket is a weapon most greatly respected
> by these people. The warriors who remained alive

fled in great disorder. No doubt they reported to their fellows that the shields they carried, though often affording protection against an arrow, cannot resist a lead bullet.

The fact is not surprising. The French muskets and pistols used .650-caliber lead bullets, which had high impact in spite of their low velocity of about 900 feet per second on account of their weight.

The three Frenchmen walked the rest of the way to the baggage camp by themselves. They arrived on January 15 to find that the Snakes had not been near it. The next day the distant mountains were enshrouded in low gray clouds, and a fierce wind began to bring with it a blizzard.

While they huddled in their tents, Louis-Joseph brought his tersely worded diary up to date. He recorded his disappointment at the inglorious ending of the Bows' march.

It is my great wish to have an opportunity to ascend those high mountains. I had been informed by the Indians that from the top of them it was possible to observe the sea in the distance. This sight would have increased greatly the value of my discoveries, for I would have been able to prepare a rough estimate of the actual distance to the coast of the ocean.

The weather improved by January 20, and on that day Louis-Joseph said good-bye to the Bow chief. He intended to carry out his father's instructions and to return eastward until he came to the Missouri River. There was no chance of going on westward into Snake country.

"Next year I hope to return here," Louis-Joseph told the chief. "You have said that this would be a good place for your people to live. Together, on the banks of yonder little stream, we will create a garden and raise grain in this rich soil."

The chief was pleased with the idea, but it is not known whether he kept the engagement. Louis-Joseph was never able to return.

Eastward out of Wyoming, past the northern flank of South Dakota's Black Hills, and across the Cheyenne River went Louis-Joseph and his companions. During their journey across the Badlands they always met with friendly hospitality from the various Indians they encountered, few of whom had seen a white man previously. Before they swung north to complete their journey to the Red River country, they camped for one night on a hilltop overlooking the junction of the Bad and Missouri Rivers. The spot was close to the site of the present-day town of Pierre. They scratched with their hunting knives a shallow hole, and there Louis-Joseph buried a lead tablet that had been given him by his father. On one side was a Latin inscription, engraved by a French craftsman, that la Verendrye had commissioned several years earlier. Apparently he first planned that his eldest remaining son, Pierre, would undertake the present journey, for it ended with the words, "Pierre Gaultier la Verendrye placed in position."

In the flickering light of the campfire Louis-Joseph scratched on the other side of the plate a rough inscription that read: "Placed by Louis-Joseph la Verendrye with la Londette and Amiotte. 1743." For some reason François's name was omitted. Perhaps he was absent in some nearby Indian village when his companions buried the plate.

Louis-Joseph began to head northward the next day while his *voyageurs* cast wistful glances at the waters of the Missouri River and yearned to be afloat. Forty-six days later they were back in Mandan country. On July 2, 1743, the four explorers reached Fort La Reine after an absence of fifteen months.

9
Last Days

The report prepared by Louis-Joseph reached Maurepas. The information he provided destroyed the optimistic hopes of that minister and his geographical advisers. Louis-Joseph must have realized the stir that he would create in France, and he took the opportunity to submit a proposal.

He wrote:

Should I be granted permission to lead another journey of exploration then I would seriously consider following the more northerly route provided by the Saskatchewan River to the west. For I am now convinced that the southwesterly direction I took on this last expedition can lead only to the Gulf of Mexico or perhaps to the Vermilion Sea (Gulf of California). Moreover, I believe that the mysterious white people of whom we have heard for so many years and from many different Indian tribes are to be identified as the Spanish who inhabit those parts.

The report written by his son brought to an end la Verendrye's career as the outstanding fur trader and explorer of New France. His health was beginning to fail, and Lamarque decided to go off elsewhere. Supplies from the Montreal traders continued to prove so unsatisfactory that Fort Maurepas, Fort Rouge, and Fort La Reine were closed down. While weeds grew around the unused doorways of those trading posts and winter snow lay piled deep outside their empty windows, the Indians resumed their former system of barter with the Englishmen of Hudson Bay.

La Verendrye returned to Quebec in 1744. He knew he was leaving that wild region of forest, lake, and river for the last time. His final letter to Maurepas reveals some of the wistful reflections that filled his mind.

Money, my lord, was always a secondary consideration with me. Although I am poorer today than I was before I began my explorations, I should consider myself completely rewarded if the care and attention I have given to the business had brought me the favor of your lordship. May I submit my claim to some reward by pointing out that I bear nine wounds on my body, that I have thirty-nine years of service in France and in this colony, and that during the last thirteen years I have endured difficulties and fatigues to create trading posts in places where no person before myself had ever penetrated. These posts will greatly increase the trade of the colony, even if no one fully succeeds in discovering any Western Sea, and in building them I did not involve His Majesty in any expense.

Beauharnois supported this letter with another one from himself. He pointed out that by the time la Verendrye had settled all his debts, the old veteran probably would have little more than $2000 left, apart from his small pension as an ensign. He wrote:

No man has done more for France's interests in this country than Monsieur de la Verendrye. I hope that you may see fit to reward him with a higher military rank in one of our militia companies, so that he may receive some adequate reward.

Maurepas experienced a twinge of conscience. A year after his return from the Northwest la Verendrye was notified that he had been granted a captaincy in the militia. This improvement in his finances enabled him to live in modest comfort at the family home on Isle Dupas, where he settled down to a restless old age with an elderly *voyageur* as his only companion.

The problem of trying to find a route across New France remained with Maurepas. The minister had begun to notice that since la Verendrye had given up his trading posts, the annual income from the fur trade was sagging. The loss had to be made up by a subsidy from the French treasury, a fact that gave no pleasure at all to the king or his ministers. Maurepas thus urged Beauharnois to appoint a successor to la Verendrye, a man who could supervise the fur trade, renew the

abandoned posts, and search anew for a way to the Western Sea.

The task was not an easy one for the governor-general. There was no sudden rush of applicants for the position. The thought occurred to the settlers along the Saint Lawrence that for all the time and energy and money he had spent in the past years, Monsieur de la Verendrye did not appear to have been treated very generously by France. La Verendrye's sons seemed to share this belief; they all had left the trading posts established by their father and returned to Montreal or gone elsewhere.

Beauharnois finally selected Nicholas Joseph de Noyelles, a forty-five-year-old native of New France with a good reputation as a militia commander and with experience in the wilds.

Noyelles lasted for two years in the Northwest. By the end of that time he decided that keeping the tribes at peace was almost a full-time job. Reliable guides remained impossible to find; trade goods and supplies continued to be a never-ending source of trouble. He resigned from his post in 1747.

Maurepas was forced at last to realize that exploration was appreciably more difficult and hazardous than he had believed. He hurriedly instructed Beauharnois to reappoint sixty-two-year-old la Verendrye.

Beauharnois did so with grim amusement. He was being proved right at last. The reappointment was almost his last official action as governor-general of New France. He was over seventy years of age and anxious to return to France. In the spring of 1748 he left at last, much regretted by the colonists he had governed so honestly.

The successor to Beauharnois was the Marquis de Jonquière. When the nobleman sailed for New France, his ship was intercepted by the British Navy. Instead of occupying the official residence at Quebec, Jonquière spent the next eighteen months in the Tower of London. He did not reach New France until September, 1749. In the meantime, his duties were performed by the Marquis Rolland Michel Barrin, a man of great good sense and integrity.

Barrin did not hesitate to tell Maurepas a few hard facts.

What has been reported to you that Monsieur de la Verendrye spent more time looking after his own interests than on exploration is entirely false. Any officers who are given that task (of exploration) will be forced to give much of their attention to commerce as long as the king shall not furnish them with any other means of support. The system may not be good but to reproach them with any slight profits they may make is a poor way to encourage them. These explorations cause heavy expense and expose a man to greater fatigue and danger than regular wars.

Unfortunately for Maurepas, King Louis had begun to take a sudden interest in documents passing through the office of his Minister of Marine and Colonies. The letter from the Marquis Barrin was one of those that the king perused. It did not increase the royal favor toward the minister. In the end Maurepas was dismissed from office late in 1748 for writing some very rude verses about the queen of France. His luxurious career was over at last.

The news of the minister's fall from grace soon reached New France. Perhaps coincidentally la Verendrye's sons returned to their beloved lakes and forests soon thereafter. Pierre became a fur trader at Michilimackinac. François settled down amiably at Fort Saint Charles on Rainy Lake. Louis-Joseph, with dreams of further exploration still active in his mind, became the first European to undertake an ascent of the unknown Saskatchewan River.

A year later Louis-Joseph wrote to his father:

> The course of this river leads directly to the west. I believe we should establish a trading post for the Crees somewhere along its upper reaches. We would spend the winter there, and when spring returns we would strike westward to find the great salt-water lake or sea.

Gray old veteran that he was, la Verendrye could not resist this final call to adventure. He sent word to his son that he would join him in the following spring and began to make his preparations at his home on the Isle Dupas.

On the evening of December 5, 1749, la Verendrye was busy in the timbered, lamp-lighted parlor of his home. He turned to a nearby table to gather up some maps that lay scattered on its surface. Suddenly his hand faltered. He swayed for a moment, and then fell unconscious to the floor. When his *voyageur* rushed to help, la Verendrye was already dead.

Two days later Pierre Gaultier de la Verendrye was buried beside Marie-Anne in Saint Anne's chapel in Montreal's church of Notre Dame. His funeral was well attended. Among the mourners were many weather-beaten old *voyageurs* who had known and worked with him during the hard and dangerous years when he had established his trading posts and driven ever deeper into the unexplored heart of New France.

Louis-Joseph never made his second ascent of the Saskatchewan River. Had he done so he might have reached the Peace River Canyon. This same route was the one that the Scotsman, Alexander Mackenzie, was to travel in 1793 and thereby become the first European to make the continental crossing.

The younger Pierre de la Verendrye died as a fur trader beside Lake Superior at the age of forty-one. François and Louis-Joseph fought against the English in the defense of Quebec in

1759, the year in which the colony became part of the British Empire.

Louis-Joseph remained independent and adventurous to the end. The English were quick to realize his abilities and offered him employment in their service. He refused their offer and likewise refused to remain in Canada now that he could no longer regard the country as his own. He sailed for France in the French vessel *Auguste* in 1761 and was drowned when that vessel was wrecked. François lived on in Quebec, apparently quite content to be ruled by the English.

La Verendrye was the last of those great French explorers who did so much to open up the vast unknown interior of the North American continent. He was unlucky, however, to have lived during a period when France's interest in her New World colony was beginning to wane. Thus, throughout his career he had to overcome misunderstanding abroad and jealousy among the French merchants in Montreal. Although he achieved less than such explorers as La

Salle and Champlain, he matched all others in his enduring courage and perseverence in the face of endless difficulties. His era ended with France's loss of New France, and even the information about his discoveries lay unheeded for over 150 years in neglected official records. Only in 1913 did his name begin to be restored to the place in history that it deserves.

In that year some schoolchildren were playing around a sand hill near Pierre, South Dakota, on a fine summer's day. A small boy suddenly noticed an unusual object lying half-buried in the earth. He picked up a small, rectangular sheet of dull gray metal. When he brushed it with his shirt sleeve, some ornate writing began to appear on the surface. On the other side of the sheet were faint scratches, which appeared to be more writing.

The children brought the plate to a local schoolmaster, who showed it to a clergyman friend. Historical authorities were consulted, and the plate was cleaned so that the engraved lettering was made legible.

One hundred and seventy years after Louis-

Joseph had scratched a hole by his campfire in the year 1743, the lead plate given to him by his father had turned up again.

The discovery was enough to set historians and geographers poring afresh over bundles of documents and reports drawn up during the latter years of the French administration of New France. La Verendrye and his son, Louis-Joseph, became fully recognized as the last of the great explorers of New France. A statue to the memory of la Verendrye stands in Quebec. His National Monument is situated close to North Dakota's New Town, where it overlooks the spreading waters of the Missouri River.

Bibliography

Burpee, Lawrence J., *Discovery of Canada*. The Macmillan Co. of Canada Ltd., Toronto, 1946

Burpee, Lawrence J., ed., *The Journals and Letters of Pierre Gaultier de Varennes De la Verendrye and His Sons*. The Macmillan Co. of Canada Ltd., Toronto, 1927

Crouse, Nellis M., *La Verendrye: Fur Trader and Explorer*. Cornell University Press, New York, 1956

Parkman, Francis, *A Half Century of Conflict*. Little, Brown and Company, Boston, 1933

Winsor, Justin, *From Cartier to Frontenac: Geographical Discovery in the Interior of North America in Its Historical Relations 1534-1700*. Cooper Square Publishers, Inc., New York, 1970

Winsor, Justin, ed., *Narrative and Critical History of America*, Vol. II. Houghton, Mifflin Company, Boston, 1886

Ronald Syme's early days were spent in an old castle in his native Ireland. Before he was nine he had the free run of the library in his home, thereby acquiring a love of reading. In later boyhood, he spent a few years in New Zealand, mostly hunting wild pig and trout fishing with his sports-loving father. At eighteen he went to sea and visited many parts of the world. About the same time he began writing short stories and feature articles. In 1934 he left the sea to become a journalist. During World War II Mr. Syme first served as ship's gunner, but later transferred to the British Army Intelligence Corps in which he saw service in North Africa, Italy, and Europe.

Today Ronald Syme, a well-known author in both England and the United States, lives in the peaceful South Pacific island of Rarotonga. His home is a century-old, white-walled stone house within two hundred yards of a beautiful lagoon. The shelves of his library are lined with books, and he can check almost any historical fact he needs for his writing. He enjoys, he says, "most of the advantages of civilization without the corresponding disadvantages."